The Power of His Blood

Manual

APOSTLE DR. JOSE ZAPICO

Our Vision

To reach the nations bringing the Word of God with authenticity, to increase the faith and understanding of all those who desire it, through books and audio-visual materials.

Published by
JVH Publications
11830 Miramar Pwky
Miramar, Fl. 33025

First Edition 2015

ISBN 1-59900-126-8

Cover art designed by: Esteban Zapico
JHV Publications - Grphic Design Department
Transciption: Tatiana Figueroa
Correction: Sarahi Leal y Lidia Zapico
Translation: Lolita DeLeon and Esteban Zapico
Impreso en USA (Printed in USA)

INDEX

LESSON 1

THE SEAL OF THE COVENANT

Genesis 9:9 *NLT*

"I hereby confirm my covenant with you and your descendants.

To study in depth the subject of God's Covenant, we must first know **What is considered as a Covenant?** The word "Covenant" in Hebrew is [*briyth*] meaning: pledge, agreement. In Greek is [*diathk*] and it refers to testament, decree. It is a term that is used in the Scriptures for the agreements:

- **Between a man and another man.** It can be between two men of equal social class or involving a lord and a vassal.
- **Between God and man.** Generally speaking, God makes a Covenant with man.

Through the Scriptures the term "covenant" most commonly describes the formal relationship between God, on the one hand, and Israel as the chosen people on the other.

In every covenant there is a mutual agreement about:
- The conditions, the privileges and...
- The responsibilities of both parties.

The Lord himself determined the provisions of the covenant: unveiled them to his people and the possibility to accept or reject it. The covenant that God made with Abraham was to cut the flesh and bleed, this act is called circumcision. In the spiritual this represents that the first thing the covenant makes, is: *cut the flesh, the flesh of the heart.* **The covenant is a commitment and who makes it, is renouncing to his sin.** God's Word is like a double-edged sword, so whoever wants to make their flesh die, let the Word of God penetrate into the depths of their inner being, because it will make a cut that separates the flesh from the spirit and cuts the desire to go on sinning. Then you can say... "*It is no longer I who live, but Christ lives in me*".

In Israel, children are circumcised eight days after berth. It is medically proven that on the eighth day that part of the body is anaesthetized, and that is the time to cut the flesh because the baby won't feel pain.

The Bible speaks of a circumcision, not only of Jewish law but of the divine law of the everlasting covenant.

I hope! All persons born again in the revelation of the New Covenant, could be baptized on the eighth day, because when the person is baptized, it is an indication in the spiritual world that they die to the world to resurrect for Christ. When someone converts, they are in full fervor of love for Christ and their flesh is anesthetized by the glory and the experience they are living. Those are the first days of spiritual life, enjoying true love with God and his presence.

Jeremiah 31:33 KJV

But this shall be the covenant that I will make with the house of Israel; After those days, saith the Lord, I will put my law in their inward parts, and write it in their hearts; and will be their God, and they shall be my people.

Throughout the ages, God has made many covenants with different men of God, equally made a covenant with a whole nation called Israel, but this "New Covenant" promised to Jeremiah, makes a new relationship possible with God and it was ratified by the blood of Christ, opening **a new pathway** that brings the new personal relationship with God.

THE SEAL OF THE EVERLASTING COVENANT IN HIS BLOOD

When the everlasting Covenant is named it refers to the New Covenant that Jesus did with his blood.

Hebrews 13:30 NKJV

Now the God of peace, that brought again from the dead our Lord Jesus, that great shepherd of the sheep, through the blood of the everlasting covenant...

The everlasting Covenant has the seal of the blood of Jesus; first he was a lamb (gave his life for the sheep) then was Pastor of pastors. By the blood of the everlasting covenant, he made you co-heirs, gave you the privilege of being children of God and it gives you eternal life.

If the covenant remains the blood also remains. It has the same capacity and has not ceased to be effective.

This blood not only confirmed the covenant, but that he really fulfilled it himself, because the stipulation of the commitment was thus: **Christ had to suffer for our sins and honor the divine law.**

To participate in the Lord's Supper, we are confirming our covenant with God.

Forgetting this covenant is to unworthily eat of the bread and the blood of Christ.

THE IMPORTANCE OF KNOWING THE COVENANT OF GOD AND ITS VALIDITY

When you have awareness of what it is to live under the **covenant**, it brings a deep passion for God and spiritual stability. You will understand that His covenant never breaks, God will not do it because He is the faithful God, which keeps the covenant and mercy; but rather, men are those who break the Covenant and are unfaithful.

Hebrews 13:20-21 KJV

[20] *Now the God of peace, that brought again from the dead our Lord Jesus, that great shepherd of the sheep, through* ***the blood of the everlasting covenant****,* [21] *Make you perfect in every good work to do his will, working in you that which is wellpleasing in his sight, through Jesus Christ; to whom be glory for ever and ever. Amen.*

The agreement which God has made with the believer, is a lifetime guarantee.

Which is the seal that certifies it? The Blood of Jesus, it is completely clean and it was shed to establish the legality of the Covenant, which is used as the seal that gives guarantee to the covenant. **The guarantee of those who live under God's Covenant.**

A will to be valid, must have a seal and a signature. The covenant of God, has a seal that establishes it and legalizes it and it's the blood of Christ shed on the cross.

- **To make the Covenant with God gives you guarantee that God** will bless you, will prosper you and will heal your land and your body, it also gives you salvation and eternal life; this is your agreement.
- **Which is yours now?** Love him above all, do not sin, obey his Word and live separate from the world and crucify every day the old nature, which is the flesh in the intentions of the heart.

Today we live under *the New Covenant in his Blood* which provides us to receive the assurance of salvation and the lasting peace.

THE COVENANT OF GOD OFFERS YOU HIS PEACE

When you know the Covenant of mercy and favor that has been poured out on your life, you will receive the peace of God. If you recognize Christ as your Savior, you cannot already be living in a state of war and internal conflict. **Your war goes against everything that tries to stop the development of your spiritual life,** but in regards to God, you have to be at peace with Him. If you are unsure of your salvation that demonstrates that you have not yet had a real encounter with the Savior.

The everlasting covenant guarantees you peace and serenity in an absolute trust in God

You cannot allow uncertainty to live inside you, in struggle because of the past, rebuke it in the name of Jesus, because when you live under *the everlasting covenant*, God gives you the certainty as a guarantee that you are God's child.

Isaiah 30:15 NLT

This is what the Sovereign Lord, the Holy One of Israel, says: "Only in returning to me and resting in me will you be saved. In quietness and confidence is your strength.

You must seek the intimacy with God and the personal relationship, regardless of the pressure surrounding you. You have to believe in the promise that Paul wrote in his letter to the Philippians:

Philippians 4:7 NLT

Then you will experience God's peace, which exceeds anything we can understand. His peace will guard your hearts and minds as you live in Christ Jesus.

When you have the revelation of the God of peace, you will be unshakable in your way of thinking, and that peace you will experience, you will not understand it, because it is more than what your mind can conceive. **Remember that God has control of all the things that occur in the heavens and below the heavens, and you who are his child, you are under this safety covering.**

Isaiah 54:10 NLT

For the mountains may move and the hills disappear, but even then my faithful love for you will remain. My covenant of blessing will never be broken," says the Lord, who has mercy on you.

When people want to fix their problems themselves, without the counsel of God; they will do so in their human strength.

For this reason, many make mistakes and rather than fixing things, they worsen them. Everything that is done in own strength, does not correspond to the level of a life that has entered into a relation with God.

No to Personal Rejection

Never despise yourself for what you are, or what you look like. In Jesus Christ there is enough beauty to cover your deformities. When Jesus sees you, He does through the covenant that covers you, which is the seal of his Blood. And when you are seen, you have an inner beauty that will exceed more than the physical. In Jesus, you're beautiful and there are enough merits, to cover your demerits. There is a legal agreement, which is the will that has been sufficiently legalized, as there is efficiency in the atoning blood of Jesus Christ. The blood of Christ is sufficient enough to wash your transgressions, sins and rebellion.

The Blood of Jesus washes your conscience of dead works from the past. The power of the Blood of Christ is efficient to give you cleansing from all your sins and sanctify you for God.

The Seal of the Covenant is Everlasting Receiving the assurance of Salvation by the Grace of the Good Shepherd

There are many people in the church who don't know if they are saved; because they don't have the security of salvation. On having known about the seal of God's covenant, you will receive the blessing of being saved by the great Shepherd. But Jesus is not only a Shepherd, He also becomes the Great Shepherd of the sheep. In the Gospel of John 10, Jesus is revealed as "*the good Shepherd who lays down his life for the sheep*", and in his surrender of love, He will shepherd you and take you to rest in green pastures. The sheep are characterized for being clumsy animals that are lost and leave the good way. For this reason the Shepherd with his staff guides the sheep, plus with the rod punishes the wolf that wants to come near the sheep to hurt them.

1 Peter 5:4 *NLT*

And when the Great Shepherd appears, you will receive a crown of never-ending glory and honor.

The Seal of the Covenant is Everlasting

The seal of the covenant does not demand that each year you present yourself in front of the presence of God to renew it, but once made God establishes it forever.

The covenant which certifies the Bible was established by the Blood of Christ,

and is and everlasting covenant

When you understand now that the covenant which God has made with you was not only for a season but it is indefinite, that gives you security and conviction that you cannot be unfaithful to the Lord, separating and forgetting Him. Your faithfulness to God must be up till death. Not just when you feel good, or when things are quiet. That should challenge you to commit to saying to God that you want to love him and be faithful every day of your life.

Your commitment is not with man, society or a system, it's with Jesus Christ. **If God says that this covenant is everlasting**, do you think that man is mortal? Why do we want an everlasting covenant if we will not be eternal? In summary then, by means of the seal of the covenant it not only made you coheir with Christ, but alike to his only begotten Son. The seal of the covenant, is an everlasting covenant because believing in Christ gives you the right to have eternal life.

LESSON 2
THE SEAL OF THE LEGALITY

The Covenant of God through the Seal of the Blood of Jesus Christ has legality.

Hebrews 13:20-21 KJV

[20] *Now the God of peace, that brought again from the dead our Lord Jesus, that great shepherd of the sheep, through **the blood of the everlasting covenant**,* [21] *Make you perfect in every good work to do his will, working in you that which is wellpleasing in his sight, through Jesus Christ; to whom be glory for ever and ever. Amen.*

When speaking of the covenant of God, it is understood that it is an agreement or an alliance established between Him and the human. Satan is the father of lies; and everything that is born of God, Satan will try to imitate it in some manner, in a distorted way. The enemy will try to make a photocopy of the original covenant of God and will demand from his followers to covenant with him through blood sacrifices; that is why the Satanists sacrifice children and human beings; to affirm this practice in them. Those covenants produce, condemnation, oppression, slavery, misery and torment.

However the Covenant of God brings life, freedom and forgiveness of sins. Its Seal affirms that it was done once and for all; through Jesus Christ

The Seal of the Blood of Christ, Makes You Immune to Sin

When a person is weak or has anemia, it is because they lack or have a deficiency of red blood cells. Their blood level has decreased, and when the person is inclined to have anemia, and that could produce infections, because the person will not have the ability to counteract certain kinds of viruses and bacteria. Such people will be vulnerable to any environmental pollution. That is why doctors recommend to them a special diet to increase red blood cells, because if not they will be vulnerable to all sorts of contagion.

In the spiritual world, **the Covenant in his Blood** seals you, delivers you from of evil and prevents you of getting contaminated, because you have high spiritual red blood cells that fight against evil.

The blood of Jesus, the son of God is a perfect blood, an impeccable and perfect DNA, and there is no contamination in it. That Blood will indicate in the spiritual world that you are heir and coheir with Christ Jesus our Lord.

The Covenant that you make with God to keep his Word and obey him, will be marked with the seal of the Blood of Christ and you will be able to enjoy its protection. He was begotten when born, but when He arose from among the dead, He was the firstborn of all who were to resurrect; that is, after Him there would be more to come. The Bible says that when Jesus arose among the dead, such was the power of the resurrection, nearly 500 people resurrected with him. This was symbol and prophetic figure of what the Lord would do in the future. That is why the Bible says that the dead in Christ will rise first.

So the Covenant can be firm, there must be blood so that it lasts. And the Blood of the Son of God is perfect.

The Blood of Christ makes us apt and accepted within the covenant; this is a firm and binding covenant, it is easier for the sky and Earth to pass than one tittle of the fulfillment of the covenant ceases to be fulfilled.

The Blood of the Son of God is life, and is effective to be applied to any sin of the human being, when he repents with all his heart.

The Blood not only confirmed the covenant, but really fulfilled it, because the condition for the fulfillment of the Old Covenant, required that for the sin to be canceled or forgiven, there had to be a sacrifice of Blood, therefore before God you can say that He has forgiven you with his Blood (that guarantees the everlasting covenant), not only covered it but removed it.

The sin kills, destroys and opens legally the doors so that they bring in the demons that operate in the life of the human beings. Christ suffered in your place, and paid the price. He was your substitute, He suffered for your sins and fulfilled before God the demands of the divine law that was death for the sin.

Jesus honored the law of the Father which was to satisfy the demand by way of the Blood.

Jeremiah 32:40 KJV
And I will make an everlasting covenant with them, that I will not turn away from them, to do them good; but I will put my fear in their hearts, that they shall not depart from me.

Did God fulfill the Covenant? Which is the part of the covenant that has to be fulfilled?, in what refers to Jesus, He pledged to suffer for us and pay for our sin, that is, the Lord chose the worst part, the most difficult which was to die for the sins of humanity. Man by divine sentence deserves to die, but Jesus said, "one moment: 'I'll will do the part of the covenant that is the worst for them, because if they die under the sentence of sin they will never have remission for their sins and crimes. If I die, taking the human form of them, then the Father will resurrect me on the third day, and they will enjoy a full and abundant life because I carried, died, and was buried with their sins, because I did not resurrects in relation to sin, but to give life to those for whom I died on the cross".

Just like Jesus died on the cross for our sins, we must go to the cross to die to sin along with Him.

Romans 6:6 KJV
Knowing this, that our old man is crucified with him, that the body of sin might be destroyed, that henceforth we should not serve sin.

The first thing that God's covenant does, is cut your flesh, your disordered appetites and sets you free from the bad habits of the fallen and sinful nature; this is when you begin to be changed into another person. It is impossible that **people of covenant** continue living in a lie, or having illicit sex, drinking or using drugs. If you keep the flesh fed by sin, you will be his slave.

Galatians 5:24 NLT
Those who belong to Christ Jesus have nailed the passions and desires of their sinful nature to his cross and crucified them there.

Jesus represented you before the Father in the very cross, so do not justify yourself of your bad actions saying: - *support me as I am.* God does not accept it, because every man and woman of covenant, should die together with Christ. Glory to God! He did not remain forever in the grave, which gave us the victory of life in the resurrection. When He arose, it was done with relation to life and life in abundance.

You're dead with Christ and buried in relation to death and sin; but also you will be raised to life in his resurrection, to have participation of his everlasting covenant.

THE GLORIOUS SIGNIFICANCE OF THE HOLY SUPPER

1 Corinthians 11:27 KJV

28 *Wherefore whosoever shall eat this bread, and drink this cup of the Lord, unworthily, shall be guilty of the body and blood of the Lord.*

To eat the Lord's Supper unworthily, is to do it without previous knowledge. Before participating of the wine, you have to ask God for forgiveness to all of your sins. Jesus will cleanse and will forgive of all iniquity when you have an attitude of repentance.

When Paul said: "*not discerning the body of the Lord*"... He was referring to the danger of approaching his table and drink of the cup that symbolizes his Blood, not believing what it represents. This does not mean that when you drink it, it will turn into blood as established by traditional religion; but that, in an act of faith you believe that this represents the sacrifice of Jesus on the cross. There are many who remain in condemnation and fear, because they have not believed that the Blood of Christ has justified them before God and they do not trust that in that Blood there is sufficient power to forgive sins.

Paul said that there were many disease among them and were weak because they did not believe in the total victory which was in the Blood of Jesus.

There are many who do not considered themselves justified before God and nor do they attempt to do so, many say they have doubts, struggles and many spiritual ties, but when you have faith in the Blood of Jesus, one of the evidences of that faith, is that you're going to enter into God's rest.

If you believe in Jesus and the Power of his Blood and his Name, your soul, your mind, your conscience will enter into God's rest at this time. You must declare "*I believe that I am saved, I believe I'm completely forgiven, I believe I am sanctified, I believe I'm healthy, because I believe in the Blood of Jesus and trust in the power of his Blood.*"

HOW YOU APPLY THE BLOOD OF JESUS OVER YOUR LIFE?

When you know what it is capable of doing and believe with all your heart by applying it with faith over your life without hesitation, the blood of Christ will be effective for your present need. You will attract the presence of God in your life. It is important that you understand that in addition to believing in the blood of Christ, you have to have a solid faith to discern the dimension of the power that it has when you apply it to your life.

1 Peter 1:18-22 *NLT*

18 For you know that God paid a ransom to save you from the empty life you inherited from your ancestors. And it was not paid with mere gold or silver, which lose their value.
19 It was the precious blood of Christ, the sinless, spotless Lamb of God. 20 God chose him as your ransom long before the world began, but now in these last days he has been revealed for your sake. 21 Through Christ you have come to trust in God. And you have placed your faith and hope in God because he raised Christ from the dead and gave him great glory. 22 You were cleansed from your sins when you obeyed the truth, so now you must show sincere love to each other as brothers and sisters. Love each other deeply with all your heart.

The power of the Blood of Christ, is the most effective power that can exist in the spiritual world just as the Scriptures which declare:

Revelation 12:11 *NLT*

And they have defeated him by the blood of the Lamb and by their testimony. And they did not love their lives so much that they were afraid to die.

There is no greater statement of faith than that which declares the power that the blood has. Here is establish the essence of the confession of a true and genuine faith, based on the Word of God and in the blood shed, whose victory has provided the eternal defeat of Satan.

Each Christian with their sins erased plus the declaration of the redemptive work of Jesus Christ through the blood, silence in a triumphant form the attempts of the prince of the darkness from intimidating God's children.

The accusing voice of the enemy, of condemnation and guilt, fades before the crushing victory of Calvary. Yes, no need to doubt at any time that the main weapon of the people of God against Satan **is the blood of the Lamb**, only it responds against all allegations that come to mind.

The true church knows and recognizes that the blood has met all charges against the redeemed, making them part of an everlasting inheritance, providing them everything necessary to live in total victory.

The blood has been an unbreakable bond of unity and relationship with God, which prevents Satan against his attempt to separate those who have been born again of the eternal and abundant resources that the God of grace offers. The principle of this central truth is that God has declared us righteous and victorious through the Blood of Jesus.

Romans 5:9 [NLT]

And since we have been made right in God's sight by the blood of Christ, he will certainly save us from God's condemnation.

You must understand the effectiveness that the Blood of Christ has sprinkled on your life; this is the only Blood that has been able to erase and clean once and for all the consequence of sin, because it was a Blood with no stain, no pollution, and without sin.

LESSON 3

THE FULFILLMENT OF THE PERFECT COVENANT

When you have a revelation of what God did with you through Jesus, you are going to give greater value to your commitment in the Christian life. Jesus was not sent into the world to establish a religion, He came to reach humanity, and rescue it from its sin through the life that emanated by his blood shed on the cross.

It was never God's desire, to give mankind a religion full of dogmas, rituals and sacraments in which human beings could not comply; God showed of Jesus Christ life and everlasting life.

When speaking about Jesus Christ, it is referred to the life because He is the very essence of life.

God resurrected Jesus Christ our Lord the great Shepherd of the sheep, by the Blood of the Everlasting Covenant. The God of peace, made the covenant in your favor; He carried your sins, and promised to suffer for them so that you do not continue under condemnation.

THE BLESSING OF THE COVENANT

Of what does this consist? In the power and the wanting; God wants to bless you and give you wonderful blessings, which is only reached by those who are part of the covenant.

The benefit was always within the reach of everyone, but to find it you must search with all your heart and desire it until it's found.

God is committed to give his rain of blessings to people of covenant.

-What does this mean? People committed, responsible, faithful, obedient and totally surrendered to God. More than everything passing that the outside world can offer you, the covenant of God rises in absolute guarantee over your life. If you are part of the covenant you must yearn to serve God.

-How do you know that a person is committed to the covenant of God? By the fact of how they serve God. No person of covenant will be passive while sitting in a church. A covenant person will be committed to serve the Lord.

-How to determine if a life has made a covenant with God? To the extent of their dedication and service to Him.

Mark 9:35 *NLT*

... He sat down, called the twelve disciples over to him, and said, "Whoever wants to be first must take last place and be the servant of everyone else."

Many today want to be great so that they can be served and not to serve. In the Kingdom of God it is different, when the greater you are the more you surrender to serve others.

Mark 10:43 *KJV*

But so shall it not be among you: but whosoever will be great among you, shall be your minister...

In the covenant there are two parts, what God is going to do and what you have to do.

When you are committed in the covenant with God it's impossible to fail and disobey him. The people who have been unfaithful in the service of God is the one who has not had ample knowledge of what is the **revealed covenant.**

Walking Under the New Covenant

Thank God for the New Covenant, because if we still lived under the old law no one would be alive today. God's law was written to let man know what sin is; if there is no law there would be no knowledge of it.

The Law of Moses was given to obey it, whether it pleased the people or not, the payment of disobedience was death.

Even today it is still the same from the point of view of sin, "*... the wages of sin is death, but the free gift of God is eternal life through Christ Jesus our Lord.*" Romans 6:23.

Anyone who breathes without Christ is dead in their trespasses and sins; I refer to spiritual death. Man never could obey God on his own account and did not find peace through the law. But in this new agreement established between the Father, Jesus the Redeemer, and the Holy Spirit, God established a New Covenant which gives commitments and benefits in a different way. God explains it this manner: *"...For I will be merciful to their unrighteousness, and their sins and their iniquities will I remember no more,* Hebrews 8:12. This text refers to when Jesus established the New Covenant, it reached Israel and the gentiles.

The New Covenant is not about laws written on tablets of stone, but laws written in the human heart. In the New Covenant God says that "never again" will He remember your sins and iniquities. That gives evidence to you, **therefore you must not permit anyone to remind you of your past and much less let the enemy hurt you reminding you of things that you did prior to this New Covenant in his blood.**

You cannot say to God: "*If you do that, I'll serve you... If you heal me, I'll serve you*" and what would happen if in the divine will of the Creator, you do not heal? Remember, God is sovereign. There are people who say... "*If God answers me this request, I am going to give all my wages to the Lord...*" and when they get paid they do not give a dime, for his work.

It is best that you say nothing and you do not promise anything to God, do not be hasty in talk and agree with God if you are not convinced of your commitment and loyalty with Him, which must go beyond a simple emotional outburst.

Many times the believers believe that God will trigger responses in their favor by what they do, forgetting that it is what God did for them.

In the Covenant with God, he says: "*I will do this, I have promised this... therefore you will do the following...*", "*I'm going to bless you, but you have to obey me*". Your obedience brings God's blessing on your life.

Man does not have to do anything to improve the sacrifice of Christ, it was made and is perfect. There is nothing to add or adjust and much less correct. You come to Jesus, accept him as your Lord and Savior as you surrender to him completely and tell him: "*thank you Lord because you did everything for me*".

Your salvation does not dependent on a man, but what Jesus did on the cross two thousand years ago. What you should do is believe and rest in Him. The same covenant depends on the great promise: *"I will not turn back of doing good to them."*

In this covenant God has pledged His Word, He has done it and is faithful to fulfill it. The Apostle Paul was right when he wrote, "that God may make us apt to do his will". Jesus wants those for which He died be: sanctified and purified in Him. **To be made apt to do his will.**

Hebrews 13:20-21 KJV

20 *Now the God of peace, that brought again from the dead our Lord Jesus, that great shepherd of the sheep, through the blood of the everlasting covenant,* 21 ***Make you perfect*** *in every good work to do his will, working in you that which is wellpleasing in his sight, through Jesus Christ; to whom be glory for ever and ever. Amen.*

The *everlasting covenant* refers to the New Covenant in his blood, which is now eternal, (in a future sense) compared to the Mosaic Covenant that was temporary and had already been repealed.

You serve God with correct attitudes, to be perfect for his service. The phrase *make you perfect,* translates to "*you prepared me*" for every good work. In Greek is /*katartizō*/ refers to the edification of the believers, because the verb refers to the notion to equip by means of adjusting, molding, restore and prepare.

We are reading that the Good Shepherd is the one that adjusts you and makes you able, enables you to do his will, it's Him who produces in you every good thing that pleases Him.

2 *Timothy 2:2* NLT

You have heard me teach things that have been confirmed by many reliable witnesses. Now teach these truths to other trustworthy people who will be able to pass them on to others.

God prepares and trains but seeks hearts available to teach others.

The word *able* means: "*sufficient in ability*"; you must understand that God will prepare and enable you, and you will be able to serve God.

It is best to be faithful serving God in one ministry rather than go through ten ministries in your local church and are unable to serve fully in any of them. Do not say: "I can't, I'm not able, I am not qualified," If you're a person of covenant, the great *Shepherd of the sheep* will make you suitable for every good work. People of covenant are not unstable, rather remain firm, able, is trained and prepared by the Spirit of God, because he knows that he must be *faithful* in anywhere placed, they have a commitment of covenant with God. **Covenant people have that yearning to be promoted spiritually.**

Covenant people do not get upset when moved to another place in the ministry, because they know that nothing belongs to them and that in the Kingdom of God there is no "personal kingdoms".

You cannot think that you will be serving God in the same position for life, until death. Don't ever be proud in your position, you must be prepared for the strategic moves that God does, because covenant people are people in movement. That is why you must sincerely ask God to be qualified, adapted, and suitable for his work and He will place you in the ministerial calling chosen for you, so you can be used by God to *the fulfilment of His will.*

Some want to run without having the ability, some want to fly without wings, but you must first let the plumage grow so you can develop flying at heights, and then you can be qualified to fly in high places.

God has to adapt you so you can be suitable to do His will.

When you love to do the will of God, you will be sanctified, because God's will is the center of success and victory. Each is sanctified for Him in the fulfillment of that will and no longer will it be your desire, but of God.

The first thing you should understand is that you will become a suitable vessel to be used by God. God cannot use you if he does not give you form, adapt you, perfect you and prepare you for what you will be doing.

God is molding you and it may be that you say: '*God...why are you making me this way?*' and He'll tell you: "*quiet, because I know what I do, you don't understand it, but I do know what I'm doing in you*"... and although sometimes you feel uncomfortable when He is adapting and molding you to be his vessel of glory, stay firm because God is working with you. Don't resist, God will shape you according to his holy purpose, because He wants to make you able and right by his divine hands.

You are able to serve God not by your personal merits but by the grace of God in his covenant.

The gifts you have are by the favor of God in your life, and has adapted you to a calling through the cleanliness and separation that is achieved only with his precious blood. There are people who want to be adapted and prepared without having been cleaned with the Blood of Christ. **There are people who are only interested in being recognized and have positions**, but they do not discerned that in the Covenant that is made with God, it is to be a clean vessel for His service.

The Holy Spirit tells you: '*I am preparing you for something you've never imagined... Don't worry about what I'm doing in others, rather worry about what I'm doing in you.*" If you feel oppressed and are uncomfortable because God is correcting an area, He tells you: *"don't fight me, do not argue with me, do not put resistance to what I do. If you're a man or woman of covenant you are going to surrender to My will, you're going to feel good for the rest of your days, and you will not feel fear, doubt or unbelief; you will feel happy for what you are, and for the manner in which I am working with you". Sometimes I have to work with your difficult character, but I will be enabling it to the order of My calling in you. Many times I have to work with your thoughts, because they are very strong. I'm going to show you the work is mine and nothing is yours, everything belongs to me, you belong to me. And I will adapt you in accordance with the model of My will."*

THE INTERNAL AND EXTERNAL SIGN OF THE BLOOD OF JESUS

Exodus 29:20 *KJV*

Then shalt thou kill the ram, and take of his blood, and put it upon the tip of the right ear of Aaron, and upon the tip of the right ear of his sons, and upon the thumb of their right hand, and upon the great toe of their right foot, and sprinkle the blood upon the altar round about.

Three places the High Priest Aaron (who ministered in the Tabernacle) had to be anointed with his sons:

1. Upon the tip of the right ear
2. Upon the thumb of the right hand

3. Upon the great toe of the right foot.

In the same manner as in all your being: your soul, body and spirit, is placed the blood of Jesus. That denotes that each member of your body, was separated for God; and all works of evil was destroyed in you. Once forgiven, there is no need to remember your past again, because the blood of Christ has completely erased your sins.

The Apostle Paul emphasizes this subject saying:

Romans 6:13 NLT

Do not let any part of your body become an instrument of evil to serve sin. Instead, give yourselves completely to God, for you were dead, but now you have new life. So use your whole body as an instrument to do what is right for the glory of God.

Every part of our body is separated and justified from sin by the blood of Christ.

If God erased all your sins, (when you repented), why does always the memory of them bring you condemnation?

If you give testimony of God to men, you can be sure that God will do the same with you. God cares for his property! You have to be sure that you belong to God because you've cost him too expensively, for you to be lost. Jesus took charge of your life, and nothing can happen to you if you live under his covering.

Psalm 91:1 NLT

"Those who live in the shelter of the Most High will find rest in the shadow of the Almighty."

This is great protection of God in the lives of his children.

LESSON 4
WHEN THE WILL IS RECOVERED

THE SEVEN PLACES WHERE JESUS SHED HIS BLOOD

The Bible says that the High Priest once a year offered a sacrifice of blood; to sprinkle it on the ark seven times. That act would forgive the sin of the people.

Leviticus 16: 14-15, 18-19, 21 NLT

14 *Then he must take some of the blood of the bull, dip his finger in it, and sprinkle it on the east side of the atonement cover. He must sprinkle blood seven times with his finger in front of the atonement cover.*
15 *"Then Aaron must slaughter the first goat as a sin offering for the people and carry its blood behind the inner curtain. There he will sprinkle the goat's blood over the atonement cover and in front of it, just as he did with the bull's blood.*
18 *"Then Aaron will come out to purify the altar that stands before the Lord. He will do this by taking some of the blood from the bull and the goat and putting it on each of the horns of the altar.*
19 *Then he must sprinkle the blood with his finger seven times over the altar. In this way, he will cleanse it from Israel's defilement and make it holy.*
21 *He will lay both of his hands on the goat's head and confess over it all the wickedness, rebellion, and sins of the people of Israel. In this way, he will transfer the people's sins to the head of the goat. Then a man specially chosen for the task will drive the goat into the wilderness.*

The things that were happening in the Old Testament were a shadow of those that would later happen in the New Testament.

This blood that was sprinkled on the *mercy seat* would have to be sprinkled seven times (the number seven has to do with abundance, fullness and integrity). The place where the priest put the blood was over the mercy seat, of which in Hebrew is */kapporeth/* which is the lid or cover of the ark of the covenant. On the *mercy seat* were sculpted in gold two cherub angels, where the glory of God descended and wrapped them.

SPRINKLED BY HIS BLOOD

The word "sprinkle" in the original Hebrew word is */zaraq/* and means: to scatter, sprinkle, toss, throw, and scatter abundantly. In the Old Testament this word is mentioned 35 times, and of them there are twenty six that has to do with sprinkling the blood upon the altar of sacrifice and Atonement. Also the word sprinkle in Greek is the root */rhantizō/* and is to sprinkle, spray, or scatter.

Just as the priest had to sprinkle on the mercy seat seven times, also Jesus Christ shed his blood in seven different occasions. Jesus as the Lamb of God and at the same time as High Priest, made a perfect sacrifice.

In each of those places He broke the various curses in which the human race had fallen. In each we can admire the marvelous work of Christ.

The Blood of Jesus is the means by which the Eternal Father has broken the curses to make you free from sin, rebellion and iniquity, to be forgiven completely.

In the Tabernacle, there were also seven places where blood was placed for the blessing of the people.

THE FIRST TIME THAT JESUS SHED HIS BLOOD

-The first time that Jesus shed his blood, was in the garden of Gethsemane.

Luke 22:44 NLT

He prayed more fervently, and he was in such agony of spirit that his sweat fell to the ground like great drops of blood.

The garden of Gethsemane was a place where Jesus frequently went with his disciples to pray. It was full of olive trees and it was at the hillside to the Mount of Olives, in front of the Temple, in Jerusalem.

What does Gethsemane mean in itself? The word means: "olive press".

In the old days, once the olive was collected it was placed in baskets to be pressed. For them was used the most traditional way of pressing olives, through a vast round rock that rolled over the olives to compress them down to grind the pulp completely, where under the enormous pressure it was crushed to drain its oil.

Luke expresses with details the great suffering that Jesus endured in the Gethsemane, comparing it as the olive when it is pressed, being completely broken and stripped of his human will. There his soul was crushed, as the process of the olive. When Jesus was in the garden of Gethsemane, He cried out and he asked his Father that if he should want, to deliver him from the suffering of death, but if it was not his will, He would take the cup and drink it obediently.

The word */gat/* is a place for pressing oil, and the word */shemar/* means oil.

In the early spring season, the olives grow in nearly all regions where it does not rain, and for this reason it becomes the symbol of the Messiah and the nation of Israel, in the spiritual sense of what is being explained now. The oil was important because it was used to anoint (Holy anointing oil) and to light the wick of the candelabra of the temple. Jesus is the light of the world.

The people brought olives during the Pentecost, to testify that it was */Adonai/*, the Lord who gave them the harvest, and not the pagan gods who had other nations.

The oil was used for anointing, for healing, for the food, for the care of the skin, to turn on the light in the Temple, to protect themselves from the sun, and more. **The oil symbolizes honor, offering burnt to the Lord, love, joy, and celebration.**

THE MESSIAH, THE CHRIST, THE ANOINTED ONE

The Messiah meant for Israel: "*the anointed with pure olive oil*", that is: *anointed with oil from the first pressing*, symbolism of what was the anointing of God. In other words, at the same time that Jesus was being pressed in Gethsemane, He was also being anointed by the Father, to emerge victorious from this difficult situation. If it had not been for that press, and the brokenness that in that place was produced in Him, He would have not been able to get to the suffering of the cross and give his life for the sin of mankind.

How do new shoots come to the silver vine? When God is pruning you, although it hurts you, it is there when you produce fruit again. It is there when new shoots come to bear more fruit. Of the Messiah it was prophesied that he would be a new shoot.

Remember, if Jesus had not been pressed as new olive, there would not have come out a branch of the great tree.

Isaiah 11:1 NLT

Out of the stump of David's family will grow a shoot – yes, a new Branch bearing fruit from the old root.

Jesus was from Nazareth, whose Hebrew word is */neser/* and means branch, like the branch that comes out when the olive tree is trimmed.

When the Father allowed for a moment, that Jesus be pressed, and the branch was pruned, at that moment a new bud was sprouting, that is you, and all those who are part of the Church of Christ.

The first place where Jesus rescued us was in the garden of Gethsemane.

What happened there? The will that man had lost was recovered. In this place thousands of years ago, Adam and Eve had given the will to the sin and to the disobedience. They were created by God and while their will was submitted to God, they lacked in nothing. They had blessing of all sorts, but the woman was deceived by the serpent and man directly disobeyed God. The snake deceived Eve because with whom he spoke to was to her, but to man, what made him lose his will was the disobedience, he preferred to give it to the desire, the yearning, to what he wanted at that time, rather than standing firm in God's perfect will.

Satan managed to steal the man's garment, which is *the coverage of God*, leaving the naked man, discovered and without protection. Not because God is at fault, but because man decided to resign the will of God choosing his own desire and his own will; and without noticing he submitted it to Satan. What gives the right to lose the original covering is the disobedience, when you mention the word "*redeemed*" it not only has to do with recovered, but with returning to the point of origin by which man was created.

In the second garden, in the garden of Gethsemane, Jesus recovered the original covering that man had lost. What is recovered is the original covering that man had lost.

With that precious blood He had the legal right to recover the lost will in man, because of the disobedience of the first man called Adam.

God did not create you to be a slave of Satan, or that you be tormented by the works of darkness and of sin; God created you so you can be a conqueror, able to exalt His Name.

When Jesus was in the Gethsemane fighting the good fight of faith, He was restoring the lost will of man. When you decide to obey God, you are rescued from disobedience and God returns to you the original state by which God had created you: To be a child of God! If you believe, it will be fulfilled in you!

Submitting the Human Will to God

The willpower that is not surrender to God is controlled by the desires of every one. When there is no willpower or self-control, the external things are going to control you.

The problem is not solved by telling a person not to do this or the other; (unfortunately it is not so easy to change the mind of a person), **he himself, must deliver his will to God by his own conviction, so he can walk in the purpose for which he was created.** When man loses the willpower to do what he believes is best for his life, there he will be guided by his disorderly passions.

Are you able to notice the grand difference? The willpower was lost in Eden, while Jesus recovered it in Gethsemane.

Remember: when He declared: "*not be done my will but yours, Father...*" He recovered the lost will, for all men who believe in Him.

WHAT WAS HAPPENING IN GETHSEMANE?

What does the writer of the Gospel of Luke mean when he speaks of drops of blood as sweat? When someone is going through a moment of fear or very intense agony or a very deep despair, the blood vessels can break under the skin, so the blood begins to escape through the pores in the form of sweat. The Bible says that from out of Jesus came sweat and blood.

It is there in that place where Jesus recovered the willpower for everyone who believes in him. It is by the Blood of Christ which you can regain the willpower to conquer the problems.

It is by the power of the Blood of Christ that has the strength to recover the will that has been lost by problems such as drugs, alcohol, rage, anger, violence, depression, and bad temper, root of bitterness, resentment, and gluttony.

All that oppresses the soul of man can be restored when he decides to believe that Jesus recovered the lost will in Gethsemane.

- **When the enemy tells you that you can earn easy money like others tell him:** "*...liar, deceiver, I rebuke you in the Name of Jesus and I cover my mind in Christ's blood and to my will of the soul to please him, because my Lord has redeemed me to surrender my life in his divine hands*".

- **When the enemy says no you cannot move on to new spiritual levels,** you must have the willpower to get up in victory through Jesus. Apply the blood of Christ in your will.

- **When the enemy is launching darts to your mind so that you fall into temptation, pray to God and tell him:** "*Lord in the Gethsemane you won the battle for me, your sweat were drops of precious blood that spilled out of your body;*" *but now I have been redeemed, and through that perfect power of victory and authority, I surrender my will to do whatever You want me to do to magnify Your name.*"

All you have to do is simple, proclaim the Blood of Jesus, and apply it over your life so that Satan does not win but that the God's will be done, even if you have to go to the cross and die over and over again, denying yourself.

If you're willing to submit to God's will, He will be with you so you act and walk in his divine will. You can't permit the enemy to control you... If this is happening to you, it is because you still have not surrendered your will to God completely.

If the enemy plays with you, it is because your will has not been surrendered into the hands of the Almighty God

When a person decides to give their will to God, the anointing that comes upon him will be powerful, and no matter what may try to come over that person, because they will be covered and protected by something so special, that it's the same anointing of the Gloria of God.

The Blood of Jesus Christ has returned to you your will, has placed you the original position in which God has created you. Jesus has broken the curse of the past that prevented you to be free, when you decide to break with these curses that were in your life, the Power of the Blood of Jesus makes you stronger and you will no longer be a slave, but will be a free person by the power and the authority of his Word and you can say:

Revelation 12:11 NLT

And they have defeated him by the blood of the Lamb
and by their testimony. And they did not love their lives so much
that they were afraid to die.

LESSON 5

A CROWN OF THORNS FREES YOU FROM RUINS

Jesus came to earth was to get you closer to God through his death. First of all so you can be saved through faith in Him, and second so that you regain the original state that Adam and Eve lost in the Garden of Eden due to disobedience.

Matthew 27:29 *NLT*

29 *They wove thorn branches into a crown and put it on his head, and they placed a reed stick in his right hand as a scepter. Then they knelt before him in mockery and taunted, "Hail! King of the Jews!"*

Genesis 3:17 *NLT*

17 *And to the man he said, "Since you listened to your wife and ate from the tree whose fruit I commanded you not to eat, the ground is cursed because of you. All your life you will struggle to scratch a living from it.*

The first couple enjoyed the abundance, wealth, mercy and kindness of God, until sadly they fell into sin. Humanity carried with the consequences of this wrongdoing before God; until Jesus came to redeem humanity from the yoke of sin through his death on the cross, and by the shedding of his blood, which wipes all evil and wickedness from the hearts.

In the garden there was no disease or poverty. When Adam obeyed God they had everything they needed.

They literally lived in a land where milk and honey flowed. God did not create man and woman to curse them, but to bless them; but sin brought as a consequence a state of curse.

Remember this: God did not create us to be cursed, but the sin opened that door upon humanity.

When Adam disobeyed God, he fell into the curse, and God had to declare judgment upon his life; and that is when also sin came upon the earth as a result of their transgression. Here not only was man affected, but animals, the ground, and even the way man would earn the fruits of their labor.

***Genesis 3:17** NLT*

And to the man he said, "Since you listened to your wife and ate from the tree whose fruit I commanded you not to eat, the ground is cursed because of you. All your life you will struggle to scratch a living from it.

Before Adam sinned, it was not decreed that the ground produced thorns and thistles; these began to germinate as a consequence of the curse.

Christ Frees Us From Ruin and Takes Us to Prosperity

Anyone who has received Christ into his heart, has been redeemed, rescued and returned to the original place in which God created man. **What redeemed man from sin and returned it to its original state, was the Blood of Christ.** There is a before and after the sin. The Blood of Christ brings redemption of sin and the curse that it produces.

If one does not recognize that the Blood of Christ has the power to redeem the life and its environment of the curse; all the earth will remain under the effect of curse. When Adam sinned he could not keep living under the effect of abundance and he had to survive with sweat, fatigue and extreme tiredness.

From that day until today, man has had to sweat for everything that he has earned in life.

Jesus shed his Blood seven times and the second time He did so was in his temple and his forehead, due to the crown of thorns placed on the head.

The Roman soldiers made the crown of the brambles encountered along the way. The act was to mock and make fun of Him saying they were going to crown the king of the Jews. This Crown was not of gold and diamonds, in fact, caused pain and ridicule, but it was the only one that, on having shed the blood, made you free from the curse of poverty.

A Crown of Thorns

The thorns of the brambles measured between 8 to 10 cm. and its thickness was 1 cm. Once they incrusted the crown of thorns, now it was not the sweat of blood that was coming from his forehead, but pure blood. The crown of thorns was the symbol of scarcity, poverty and misery. This was placed on the head of Jesus, representing the sin, the curse of the land (... *It will grow thorns and thistles... Genesis 3:18*), and the only thing powerful enough to break that curse, was not the crown of thorns, but the blood of Christ.

When the thorns pierced the head of Jesus, they were freeing humanity from the curse of poverty. The man had received poverty from Adam's sin, but was now receiving the redemption of poverty, through the crown of thorns placed on Jesus.

This promise would come to all who believed in that blood. What Satan wanted to use for evil, God would use it for the good of those who love him. When the soldiers took those thorns (without knowing it) they were doing a prophetic act.

By the power of this Blood not only the power of the curse of poverty was broken, but those who today claim his Blood are anointed to be free even from negativity, from failure, from defeat and all evil that the enemy has placed through captivating thoughts in the depths of the mind of every human being.

2 Corinthians 8:9 NLT

You know the generous grace of our Lord Jesus Christ. Though he was rich, yet for your sakes he became poor, so that by his poverty he could make you rich.

The birth of Jesus in a manger, was not to teach us poverty, because Jesus wasn't poor. He came from the immensity of heaven where there were riches and abundance of all things. **If you gather all the riches of the land, they would not compare to what Jesus had in heaven.** Joseph was not a poor a person who would not pay a hotel so that his wife could give birth, but all the places were occupied; and with that, it was demonstrated that man is often too selfish to give Jesus a place in his life and heart.

ABUNDANCE FOR THE ONE WHO WANTS IT

John 10:10 NLT

The thief's purpose is to steal and kill and destroy. My purpose is to give them a rich and satisfying life.

Having life in abundance means you're going to live in the expectant land, not only of the now but of eternity. Who are those riches prepared for? For the sinner, or for the righteous? Every believer redeemed by the Blood of Christ has made a blood covenant with Jesus to go from the curse of poverty to an abundant life. You have to be ready to receive all that God said that you should have. Where does poverty come from, God or the devil? Scarcity brings misery, and poverty is a cause of sin.

Malachi 3: 10 *NLT*

"Bring all the tithes into the storehouse so there will be enough food in my Temple. If you do," says the Lord of Heaven's Armies, "I will open the windows of heaven for you. I will pour out a blessing so great you won't have enough room to take it in! Try it! Put me to the test!

- **Why does God say he will open the windows of heaven?**

The word window, in the original Hebrew word is "floodgates". The correct text should be this: "*I will open the floodgates of heaven*" instead of "windows". The floodgates of heaven will always be closed when people do not give God what belongs to him; God said: *test me on it*. It pleases God to shed many blessings upon his children, because He is good and full of mercy. Try Him and you will receive your blessing! The second meaning of the word floodgate in Hebrew is, ambush; that is "test me in this, and I will prepare an ambush, against this enemy which has detained the blessing I want to give you".

God will prepare an ambush with his angels to protect your harvest and your goods from all evil attack.

Previously some councils maintained the doctrine that poverty is the symbol of Christian humility. You must understand, that poverty is part of a curse and it is not the will of God to suffer necessity without cause. Jesus taught: ***"Give, and it shall be given unto you; good measure, pressed down, and shaken together, and running over".***

Why are there people who always like to receive and never like to give nothing? When you learn to give what little you have, you will receive the much that heaven has reserved for you, and you shall never be scarce; God blesses the giving hand! God does not suffer from deficit or is bankrupt!

Psalms 50:12 *NLT*

If I were hungry, I would not tell you, for all the world is mine and everything in it.

Poverty should not be part of you! That is why you should not accept it, because it does not come from God. The blessing is part of God's plan, if you're a giver and a grateful sower, always reap the abundance that will make you prosperous in its time.

The enemy in the Word of God is recognized as a thief. Sometimes it is not that God does not want to bless you, it's that the thief is stealing the fruit and you don't know how to rebuke it.

When you recognize that it cannot be part of your Christian life; (because you are a child of God under the Covenant) you should fight the battle of faith, and start to claim the promises of blessing of prosperity and abundance that God has for your life. **Remember:** Did Jesus give Peter, a miserable fishing or an abundant fishing? The net was braking from the many fish right? So God is good.

THE BLESSING OF WORK

There are people who believe that work is a curse because it does not come from God; (perhaps that's why there are so many lazy people who don't like to work). When Adam was placed in the Garden of Eden, it was for him to labor it and live from it in abundance; however, when Adam stopped doing what he had to do, he fell into disobedience. Don't stop working because God gives you the strength to do it, nor stop working for God, because that gives you the blessing of heaven and rain in its time.

So if you are faithful in your work, keep your testimony, and give your tithes and offerings, you'll be prospered with the blessing of God

The world functions based on Mammon, the god of *temporary riches of this world*, and many are those who make a covenant with Satan to obtain it, but their soul falls into disgrace and captivity, under the prison of its claws.

Instead, believers operate based on the law of redemption, and the prosperity of the "*lasting riches*". With the shed blood of Christ on his forehead (due to the crown of thorns), Christ redeemed you from the curse of poverty braking it forever in your life.

If you are faithful to God in your tithes and offerings, He says he will rebuke for you, the devourer of your finances. The devourer will try to surprise you, but God will ambush the devourer.

LESSON 6
THE FLOGGED BACK TO GIVE HEALTH

The third place where Jesus shed his blood was in the yard where Roman soldiers whipped him by order of the Procurator Pontius Pilate. This happened when they tortured him, whipping him thirty-nine times before going to the cross. Whenever the whip hit him, it tore his flesh, making blood gush from his back.

Isaiah 53:4 NLT

Yet it was our weaknesses he carried; it was our sorrows that weighed him down. And we thought his troubles were a punishment from God, a punishment for his own sins!

Matthew 27:26 NLT

He ordered Jesus flogged with a lead-tipped whip, then turned him over to the Roman soldiers to be crucified.

When the Romans whipped a prisoner it was to almost kill him; on the fortieth lash there was the possibility that the person died inevitably. However, as it was prophesied that Jesus died on a tree and not by lashes, (in that hellish beating), did not succumb. At that time the prophecy of Isaiah was fulfilled when he said:

Isaiah 53:4 NLT

...it was our sorrows that weighed him down. And we thought his troubles were a punishment from God, a punishment for his own sins!

When the Romans punished prisoners with lashes, it would break the skin, muscles and tissues; each whip given to Jesus was breaking the curse of disease which had come as a result of sin.

It had been discovered that there are thirty-nine diseases called "basic" from which all other diseases that exist are derived from. Each lash was providing healing for each disease. Each of the diseases was defeated by the Blood coming out of the sores on his back.

What does the word sore mean? The word "sore" means: bruise, stripe, wound. So it is important that you understand that when you pray: "*...with his stripes we are healed*", you are proclaiming, that for the beating that tore the whipped back of Jesus, you're healthy!

The whip with which struck Jesus consisted of several strips of loose or braided leather of different lengths, in which they had tied at intervals balls of iron or sharp pieces of bone of sheep, with a piece of lead at the tip. When the Roman soldier whipped vigorously the back of Jesus the iron balls caused deep bruises and the bones of sheep from the leather strips cut the skin. His back was made a sore! **Some deny today that God can heal, however, in Hebrews it is written:**

Hebrews 13:8 ***NTV***

Jesus Christ is the same yesterday today, and forever.

Denying that Jesus heals today, is to override all that Jesus suffered in his body, when he took our place and suffered whipping until he became sore. You can't deny it, because to do so is to deny that the Covenant of Jesus is real. We know that Jesus is God's truth.

Redemption not only has to do with being forgiven, but to be healed. Salvation is in every sense, integral health.

Jesus surrendered voluntarily so that the whip could flog his back, and as a result, you and I are healthy.

One of the prayers that saddens the Lord is when we tell him: "*heal me Lord if it be your will...*" He did not suffer the whip of Rome, nor was his back lashed thirty-nine times in vain; these open sores give health every time you believe with all your heart.

James 1:6 ***KJV***

But let him ask in faith, nothing wavering. For he that wavereth is like a wave of the sea driven with the wind and tossed.

When you're going through a moment of pain and illness, remain quiet and calm before the Lord. Your health is not based on your personal effort, but on what He did for you.

The firm believer in Jesus is a solid person, who knows who its Savior is and what God did for him, that is why he cannot be double-minded.

Can God heal you? Yes and of any disease. Your health is important, because He made a covenant of blood for you. The price of your health was paid two thousand years ago. What you have to do is extend your hands and take the healing by faith, receive what He already did for you on the cross.

Everything that God has already done for you, you must appropriate it and enjoy it because it belongs to you.

You need to believe that God wants to heal you now, because while you are alive you will have a limited body that gets fatigued, and which is constantly battling against viruses and bacteria; it is at this point that you need the powerful blood of Christ over your life.

Remember that everything can fail, but your Heavenly Father who expressed his love through Jesus, will never fail you and will never abandon you.

When you get on a plane and you sit in the seat assigned; that aircraft can be nine hours in the air. You have to have faith and believe that you will arrive without any problem to your final destination. Although you may not know the pilot, and do not know whether the plane has any mechanical faults or not; you feel confident that everything will be fine. If that happens with a plane and a pilot that you don't know, think how much more you can trust when you put your life in the hands of him who is the owner of the universe. You must trust in God and His Word, and believe like a child in the power of the blood of Christ.

Salvation begins with the forgiveness of sins, but does not stop there, continues with health, deliverance, freedom, baptism of the Holy Spirit and prosperity.

To be forgiven, is the master key to begin to enjoy what comes from there onwards through Jesus Christ.

Christ the Healer

Luke 13:10-13 NLT

*10 One Sabbath day as Jesus was teaching in a synagogue, 11 he saw a woman who had
been crippled by an evil spirit. She had been bent double for eighteen years and was
unable to stand up straight. 12 When Jesus saw her, he called her over and said, "Dear
woman, you are healed of your sickness!" 13 Then he touched her, and instantly she could
stand straight. How she praised God!*

This woman was sick for eighteen years, by a degenerative disease in the bones of her back, perhaps suffering from muscular dystrophy; but to Jesus the medical diagnosis didn't matter; He saw her and said: "*Woman, you are healed of your sickness!*" When the Lord saw the woman, He did not speak to her, He spoke to the spirit of sickness, which was causing that problem.

Many times we don't have to pray, but rather must speak to the spiritual problem that is causing the bond or specific sickness, firstly bind it and then order it in the Name of Jesus that it must leave immediately from that body.

If you are going right now through a test of pain and illness, I encourage you to fight the fight of faith; take your legal right to which you belong, and pray so that by his stripes on his whipped back, you are healed. He took your pain, your whip, your sickness, your wound, so you don't have to keep carrying it. This is a matter of faith.

Do not be angry with God for what is happening to you; believe in the promises of God, and fight for your blessing.

The Bible teaches us that "*the devil is the one who steals, kills and destroys*", but it pleases God in blessing those who believe in him. The price of your health has been paid. If for some reason you are ill, injured or weak, Satan is invading a property that long ago was paid for. You are a paid, not owed property. The enemy cannot require from you nothing. You've been bought by Jesus Christ. Your body belongs to Jesus.

You must take authority and pray with faith: "*by the Blood of Christ I have been redeemed from the curse of sickness, and bind the spirit of sickness, ordering it out of my body and do not ever enter in the Name of Jesus, because this body is not yours*". Remember that your health was bought by the whipping on the back of Jesus.

There is another example in the Bible that is important that we read it at this time:

Mark 9:17-23 NLT

17 *One of the men in the crowd spoke up and said, "Teacher, I brought my son so you*
could heal him. He is possessed by an evil spirit that won't let him talk. 18 *And whenever*
this spirit seizes him, it throws him violently to the ground. Then he foams at the mouth
and grinds his teeth and becomes rigid. So I asked your disciples to cast out the evil spirit,
but they couldn't do it." 19 *Jesus said to them, "You faithless people! How long must I be*
with you? How long must I put up with you? Bring the boy to me." 20 *So they brought*
the boy. But when the evil spirit saw Jesus, it threw the child into a violent convulsion,
and he fell to the ground, writhing and foaming at the mouth. 21 *"How long has this been*

happening?" Jesus asked the boy's father. He replied, "Since he was a little boy. [22] The spirit often throws him into the fire or into water, trying to kill him. Have mercy on us and help us, if you can." [23] "What do you mean, 'If I can'?" Jesus asked. "Anything is possible if a person believes."

The back of Jesus had not yet been whipped, and the Covenant had not been signed when the Lord made this healing but he was already working for what he had been sent. Jesus did not raise an eloquent prayer for the child; He only called the sickness by its name and cast it out.

To pray, to cry out and fasting is done "before" facing a spiritual battle.

The sickness is not just prayed, it's commanded in the Name of Jesus. What happens is that the level of faith has to increase in the heart, so that God's gifts are activated at this time, for the blessing of lives. There are many people who believe that they are not healed because the Pastor of their church did not say a very long prayer; what you need is to believe in the Word of faith to receive the healing.

What heals is the anointing of God together with faith. When there is an anointing of miracles, healings, signs and wonders and you enter into that move, simply believe that you're healed and you will receive your miracle.

When the woman with the flow of blood touched the hem of the garment of Jesus, she was healed at that moment. Not only did the power come out from Jesus to heal this woman, but when the flow in her stopped, she returned to her normal life. That is wonderful! Her economy was restored, because everything she had was spent on doctors. The Lord returned what the devil had stolen from her, because she put her faith in the author of health.

LESSON 7
THE PIERCED HANDS THAT RESTORES YOUR AUTHORITY

In the previous lessons, I have mentioned the word "REDEMPTION" since its action is intimately linked to the blood of Christ, as the "price of a ransom". I want to study in depth into this so you have clear the work that Christ realized for the redeemed.

The word redemption means: **rescue and return things to their original state with which God created them.** The Lord did not create man to be slave of sin, and by consequence of this to Satan, but to be free people, with a heavenly destination. The word "redemption" has another meaning and has to do with **buying a slave for price**. The man and the woman had fallen under the bondage of sin, and the enemy had them captive like slaves to his service. Christ had to pay a high price to remove each one from the market of the slavery to sin, and this price was his valuable blood.

1 Peter 1:18-19 *NLT*

18 *For you know that God paid a ransom to save you from the empty life you inherited from your ancestors. And it was not paid with mere gold or silver, which lose their value.*
19 *It was the precious blood of Christ, the sinless, spotless Lamb of God.*

The Fourth Place Where Jesus Shed His Blood

Through his pierced hands, he oozed blood in abundance. When soldiers pierced his hands with nails to hang him on the cross, which was already prophesied thousands of years ago by King David. As it was written in Psalm 22:16, when he says: ...*For dogs have compassed me: the assembly of the wicked have inclosed me: they pierced my hands and my feet.* The psalmist was prophesying the horrible form of suffering of which Christ shed his blood. The hands that healed the sick, blessed the children and raised the dead, those blessed and pure hands were pierced so that redemption would sprout, for you and for me. The hands feel, caress and touch, but it is also the instrument of labor to receive the daily goods. Jesus was being injured in his hands, so that the man receive prosperity.

THE PROMISE OF PROSPERITY IN THE LABOR SERVICE

Genesis 1:27-28 *NLT*

27 So God created human beings in his own image. In the image of God he created them;
male and female he created them. 28 Then God blessed them and said, "Be fruitful and multiply. Fill the earth and govern it. Reign over the fish in the sea, the birds in the sky, and all the animals that scurry along the ground."

Here God reveals to you that everything He created was for man to govern it. All the authority and all the dominion was placed in the hands of man, in this case of Adam and Eve who was the first couple that God put in the Garden of Eden. But when Adam disobeyed God that authority was removed from him and Satan becomes the god of this world. At that time it was Satan who gave the orders, and what man did was not what God wanted, but what the enemy wanted. Satan stole the dominion and the authority, from man.

When Jesus was crucified he shed his blood, so that you recover the lost dominion and were prosperous in everything you undertake.

The nails embedded in his hands were achieving that to you be returned the dominion and the authority that the man had lost. Christians are fleeing from the enemy and they are afraid of him, because they don't understand the total victory of Christ on the cross. The redeemed live in obedience and victory because of that blood which guarantees the lost prosperity. The hands of Jesus were not pierced by chance. No! Those hands were pierced for the sin of man.

No matter how much wickedness or opposition we find, we have the authority and dominion in the Name of Jesus, to make him offensive and to destroy what the devil wants to do for evil.

Mark 16:18 *KJV*

They shall take up serpents; and if they drink any deadly thing, it shall not hurt them; they shall lay hands on the sick, and they shall recover.

It's time to believe that God breaks all the iniquity over yours, in the mighty Name of Jesus. Pray for your son, nephews and declare that though perhaps they are far or are rebellious, they will serve God.

If your spouse is not yet saved, don't lose hope, reclaim the blood of Christ over him and take authority over any kind of wickedness, because the Lord returned to you the dominion of the authority of his Name in your hands.

Taking the Proper Authority in His Name

Pray this way for your children: "*by the Blood that in the hands of Jesus Christ was shed on the cross of Calvary, and for the dominion that has been returned to me, I reclaim that no evil can touch them and that no teachings outside the will of God in School, College, or University can progress in their mind, in the Name of Jesus*".

In the moment you take authority over the enemy, you will see that God's promises are beginning to become a reality. Remember: everything in which you put your hands, God will make it prosper. Not by any ritual, but because the authority has been returned in our hands through the Blood of Jesus. He surrendered voluntarily, and his hands were being nailed, the dominion returned to the hands of all those who one day believed that the dominion returned to their hands through the sacrifice of Jesus.

Remember: Our whole life revolves around a plan and a purpose of God. Your hands now are your hands in the earth, they cannot be placed anywhere, nor should they touch the filth, such as magazines or pornographic videos, fraudulent money and all that comes from lying. Your hands are to bless, to pray for the sick, to serve the poor, to unleash the dominion of Christ to the earth.

Think about this, if the devil would have understood the cause by which the hands were pierced, he would have never allowed the Roman soldiers to pierce them with nails. If he had understood he would have not permitted it. That is why the church has the authority to bind and loosen, in the Name of Jesus and by the blood shed through his hands, you have the right to reclaim everything that the enemy stole from you.

When you're facing an illness or a satanic opposition, he will not see just any hands, but hands with dominion and authority over the situation.

When you see your hands, pray to the Lord that He give you hands to demonstrate the Majesty of God wherever you go. Everything that your hand touches be changed, prospered, be impacted, because my hands have power, dominance and authority to recover, what the devil has wanted to steal and remove for so long. You will declare that everything that God puts in your hands will be blessed and prospered.

Joseph was a young man who since childhood had the favor of God on his life, was humble and obedient, believed the promises of God faithfully, the Word says "that God was with him", that lead him to become a prosperous man in everything he did.

Genesis 39:3 *KJV*

And his master saw that the Lord was with him, and that the Lord made all that he did to prosper in his hand.

Break the boundaries, do not believe in little, let nothing stop you, you can do everything that comes into your hands, because God wants to bless you.

We can do all things through Christ who strengthens us and have dominion in our hands, to establish the purpose of the Kingdom of God in every dimension of his glory. To do what God says you have to do, God will bring a level of resource to your life because the enemy knows that over your life, there is authority and dominion to reach what God has for you. You have to stay faithful believing God that everything you touch will be prospered and blessed.

Receive this Word of God for your life and believe that as it was with Joseph it will also be with your life.

They will come over you, anointing of wisdom and of knowledge. God still will give you creative ideas so that you begin to develop projects that God himself will place within you. He'll give it to you because you have a heart for planting in the Kingdom.

Don't Envy the Work of Others

The hammers that drove the nails in his hands and feet were just instruments, but were not the culprits. A hammer is a tool, it can be used to lift or to destroy. We cannot blame the hammer that the wood is not well aligned, it is simply a tool in the hands of who used it.

For this reason, the Bible says that the battle is not against flesh and blood, but against evil spirits; and many times in the church, the brothers in faith, will hammer each other rather than edify.

LESSON 8

THE FEET THAT GIVE YOU SECURITY IN THE WALK

THE FIFTH PLACE WHERE FROM JESUS BLOOD FLOWED

The fifth place where his blood flowed was on his feet. The manifestation of his blood shed in this place of his body was also a prophetic act, which was fulfilled as it had been declared.

Psalms 22:16 [KJV]

For dogs have compassed me: the assembly of the wicked have inclosed me: they pierced my hands and my feet.

Genesis 3:14-15 [NLT]

14 *Then the Lord God said to the serpent, "Because you have done this, you are cursed more than all animals, domestic and wild. You will crawl on your belly, groveling in the dust as long as you live.* 15 *And I will cause hostility between you and the woman, and between your offspring and her offspring.* ***He will strike your head, and you will strike his heel."***

Where does the first Gospel proclamation exist? In the book of Genesis. At the time in which the Lord established judgment in Eden and described the consequences of sin, it also gave a prophetic word to redeem mankind.

In the previous text you have read that God would put hostility between Satan and the woman, between his offspring and her offspring. The promise consisted in the following: "*He will strike your head, and you will strike his heel*". Hurt the head of Satan, that is: bruise, break, which alludes to the long struggle between good and evil, which God wins at the end through Jesus Christ, the second Adam.

Jesus suffers the effect of that wound made on the heel, upon being broken by God and wounded at Golgotha and on the cross, for our sins.

The Lord, on bruising the serpent at the same time indicated he would destroy the inherited curses because of it, and although the offspring of

the woman would be hurt and wounded on the heel, left the promise of victory over sin.

Here you can see a dual prophecy; God is cursing the natural snake (animal), and also speaks to the spiritual snake (Satan) which is the Old Serpent or Devil. In the middle of the judgement, God brings a glitter of hope. Before Adam was expelled from Eden, God was already giving the promise of deliverance for humanity; the offspring of the woman (who was Jesus) would defeat the *Old Serpent*. While this, might only hurt the heel of Jesus, how would it be done? Making him suffer, causing suffering and pain.

This verse contains the first proclamation of the Gospel. Here we find in summary form, the richness, mercy, pain and glory of the redemptive work of Christ, (the offspring of the woman). The promise would be conceived divinely but at the same time it would be completely human.

When God pronounced: ***"And I will cause hostility between both offspring's"***, it's because the Lord cursed the spiritual snake (Satan) declaring that it would be crushed by the power of God through the offspring of the woman, which was Jesus Christ.

This prophetic message of Genesis 3, is good news for the man, as God would do the unspeakable to recover the human being that he had lost.

The first serious struggle of offspring's, such as Jesus told the religious who did not accept him as God: *...For you are the children of your father the devil*, which is your offspring does not come from God. Paul for example says to the believers in Rome:

Romans 16:20 NLT

The God of peace will soon crush Satan under your feet.

The battle began not in heaven but in Eden, from there it continued to the earth, where Jesus defeated Satan, (and ultimately will defeat the evil one in the end of the reign of the Antichrist).

The Power Delegated to the Church to Tread on Serpents and Scorpions

The word "tread" in Hebrew is */darak/* and means: "walking, marching, trample". The word "to tread" appears sixty-two times in the Old Testament and means: "an intense way of knowing where we are walking". His victory is delegated to those who believe, the Church becomes part of the victory of Christ. That is why Jesus Christ delegates authority to his disciples over the powers of evil. They are still there but the believer has authority over them. "ALL THINGS ARE POSSIBLE TO HIM THAT BELIEVES."

Luke 10:19 KJV

Behold, I give unto you power to tread on serpents and scorpions, and over all the power of the enemy: and nothing shall by any means hurt you.

God delegates the authority of Christ to his beloved Church to step on to take back. We can see the promise of possessing many years ago, given by God to Moses and his people.

Deuteronomy 8:1 NLT

Be careful to obey all the commands I am giving you today. Then you will live and multiply, and you will enter and occupy the land the Lord swore to give your ancestors.

Treading, is to take possession of what God has delivered. For you to take possession of something in the spiritual world, you must believe and trust in this promise; exercise dominion over the territory that God has promised belongs to you. The word “possess” appears 116 times in the OT and in Hebrew is: */yarash/*. It is a word rich in meaning: take possession of and to inherit. God promises to give to Israel Canaan as eternal possession. To the Church is given the promise to go into all the world preaching the good news.

The Blood Shed in His Feet Give you Security in Your Walk

The Blood shed in the wounds of his feet, also redeemed you from your lack of dominion, security and authority; because when Adam fell into sin, he lost the spiritual dominion which was together with its stability and security.

Man was created to be the head and crown of the creation. The feet of Jesus, and his injuries returned to you that dominion, which the first man lost.

God promised his people they would always be spearhead, in which they would take possession of a good land and never be taken out of there.

Deuteronomy 28:13 NLT

If you listen to these commands of the Lord your God that I am giving you today, and if you carefully obey them, the Lord will make you the head and not the tail, and you will always be on top and never at the bottom.

That was the promise to his people, however, they doubted and provoked God to anger with their disobedience and idolatry.

- The Lord gave this dominion to Adam and he lost it.
- He gave it to Israel and they lost it,
- Now He gives it to the Church of Christ, do not lose it, use it!

Thanks to the blood shed from the feet of Christ, you are receiving the dominion that was lost.

If you have an attitude of gratitude towards the shed blood of Jesus, you will be acknowledging what his feet did for you and that is why you should never again allow to be stepped on by Satan.

The Lord is willing to accompany you and to be with you at all times; He says in his Word: "*I will not leave you nor forsake you*". He gave you authority on your feet, so that wherever you go there exists no power of the enemy that can stop you, because you have been redeemed by the Blood of Christ.

You have authority to bind the devil in your neighborhood, in your work and in all places where needed to subdue him.

You have a powerful investiture in the spiritual world and Satan knows what kind of covering you have, he also knows if you live in Holiness or if you are naked; so you have the legal authority to say: "*devil, move back, I reclaim my neighborhood for Christ*".

You have to reclaim the blood of Christ on your family, and place it on the doorposts of your house and the bedrooms of your children in an act of faith. A good way to pray is: "*I declare that the Blood of Christ is on the doorposts of the house, and nothing that is not of God can enter my home, so that when the spirit of wickedness and destruction want to enter, they will see the Blood of Christ and leave fleeing.*"

It is time to recover what the enemy has stolen from you and consecrate it forever for God's work. You are an heir of salvation; you are not beneath anything but above the circumstances. Over what should you take authority? In everything that rises against the real power of God.

LESSON 9

THE OPEN SIDE WHERE THE CHURCH WAS BORN

OF THE WOUNDED SIDE OF JESUS, CAME OUT BLOOD AND WATER

***John 19:31-34** NTV*

[31]It was the day of preparation, and the Jewish leaders didn't want the bodies hanging there the next day, which was the Sabbath (and a very special Sabbath, because it was the Passover). So they asked Pilate to hasten their deaths by ordering that their legs be broken. Then their bodies could be taken down. [32] So the soldiers came and broke the legs of the two men crucified with Jesus. [33] But when they came to Jesus, they saw that he was already dead, so they didn't break his legs. [34] One of the soldiers, however, pierced his side with a spear, and immediately blood and water flowed out.

It was already afternoon and Jesus had been suffering for six consecutive hours. The priests did not want his body on the cross because the next day was the day of "resting" and could not perform any work. The order was given to break the bones of the legs of the crucified and thus death was faster. The Jewish law, could not tolerate that someone remained on the cross during the night, the next day it was obligatory to do nothing, so the soldiers had to lower them before the sun sets; so that the curse was not transferred to the land; since the law said that everyone who died on a cross, could not be there on the day of rest, because if not the curse of the crucified fell upon it.

***Psalm 34:20** NLT*

For the Lord protects the bones of the righteous; not one of them is broken!

According to the Roman customs of the crucifixion, they left the condemned on the cross an average of five or six hours while he was tortured; then they broke their knees and it was there when finally the crucified expired. The soldiers broke the bones of the prisoners who were being crucified next to Jesus, and when it was the Lord's turn, He was already dead, the soldier had no need of breaking the bones of the legs of Jesus, but he did pierce his side with his spear. (This was also a prophetic sign).

John 19:32-37 *NLT*

"So the soldiers came and broke the legs of the two men crucified with Jesus. But when they came to Jesus, they saw that he was already dead, so they didn't break his legs. One of the soldiers, however, pierced his side with a spear, and immediately blood and water flowed out. (This report is from an eyewitness giving an accurate account. He speaks the truth so that you also may continue to believe.) These things happened in fulfillment of the Scriptures that say, "Not one of his bones will be broken," and "They will look on the one they pierced."

When someone died on the cross, his suffering agony stretched for hours on end.

There came a moment in which the body of Jesus could not be sustained anymore because of the weakness and the lack of water and blood in his body, that caused for the lungs to close preventing him from breathing. But suddenly was heard a weak voice that said: "*Father, into your hands I commend my spirit*".

When the soldier came to break the legs of Jesus, he was already dead and there was no need to do so, so that the Scriptures are fulfilled.

THE OPEN SIDE OF CHRIST

But to be sure, he took his spear and pierced his body. When his side was opened and his heart pierced by the Roman spear, blood and water came out. **The Church of Christ was being born of the water of the Spirit of God.** After being convinced that he had lost his life according to the mandate of the law and that the body was already dead, nothing could satisfy the human cruelty but until his heart was pierced with the spear. Let's see, now, perhaps the soldier who pierced the side of Christ was not a suitable example - while repugnant - of our sinful race? And perhaps his heartless act was not a type of our stubborn irreverence?

Also many today, after the death of the Savior continue piercing his body. How do they achieve it?

- **Denying or doubting** his Deity,
- Giving him **discredit** to his testimony and his doctrine teaching another gospel.
- Those who **refuse to believe** in his capability of Savior and forgiver of sins.
- Being **indifferent** to his sacrifice and death, rejecting his call.

It is interesting to understand that the first five times that Jesus shed his Blood, had to do with the exterior of the man: will, prosperity, dominion, security, and stability. Now, these last two places where Jesus shed his Blood had to do with the internal.

The spear goes beyond the visible part, entered into his side as if saying: He came to shed his Blood and to heal the wounded soul of the people. What we see now is an open side, a spear entering in his interior. It has been estimated that the human body has four liters of blood. When the side of Jesus was opened it shed the last remnants of his blood with water. Jesus had already announced it, when he said: *I came to shed My Blood to forgive sins once and forever.* When you receive the benefits of his death remember that **Jesus heals your spiritual and physical sickness.**

Let the Lord heal your pain, those who still have not been cured, because if you don't, it will be converted into bitterness and later into hatred, which will then be a demonic spirit that will oppress your soul.

You must understand that your battle is not against any human being, your war is not against flesh and blood, the main war is against principalities and hosts of wickedness (Ephesians 6:12); people are instruments in the hands of God or the devil, and you have to stand firm against that demon that can be acting behind that person to resist it in the Name of Jesus.

When his side was opened, he stopped the curse so that the bitterness would never reach you nor that hate would oppress you. Jesus reversed the curse and healed the pain, now he invites you to take it because it is at your disposal. Once healing is produced in your soul, you'll never feel the pain of the wound that bears the fruit of resentment.

Jesus not only delivered you, healed you and rescued you, but he recovered the original state by which God had created you. When you understand how He gave everything to the Father, it is easy to love him for everything he did for you and me. How will not the Father give you what you ask, if he gave what he loved the most?

2 Corinthians 5:17 NLT

This means that anyone who belongs to Christ has become a new person. The old life is gone; a new life has begun!

If the demons had understood what it meant to open the side of Jesus the Roman soldier would of never pierced him. Although the Roman soldier and the demons did not understand the mystery of the cross, now you understand it, because Jesus loves you, and through its open side, made you part of his Church.

Man Experienced in Brokenness

A prophecy that still had not been met, is that of Isaiah, but in that glorious moment, the time came to do so. He had come to heal the brokenhearted by his open side; so that the believer would no longer be sad, nor with an ailing soul, because He changed the mourning into dance.

Isaiah 61:1 [NLT]

The Spirit of the Sovereign Lord is upon me, for the Lord has anointed me to bring good news to the poor. He has sent me to comfort the brokenhearted and to proclaim that captives will be released and prisoners will be freed.

Actually Jesus was anointed with the power of God not only to heal the disease and break the chains of oppression that Satan had placed on mankind, but that also Jesus Christ removed burdens and yokes, healing the brokenhearted.

God wants his people to live in an attitude of continuous joy and not in anguish, exhaustion and the emptiness you get while living a life in sin separated from God. Jesus experienced the brokenness, not only in his death on the cross, but through his own ministry.

He went through the pain of betrayal and rejection of all those He loved and those that He called his friends. The priests and scribes were those who wanted to crucify him, because they knew that the only thing able to save them from that situation was a dead Jesus.

All that broke the heart of Jesus as a human, and He felt what you could feel in a similar situation. He was the Son of God and at the same time was God, but also as a man felt the pain. What Jesus suffered on the cross was not easy, because he bore all the sins of mankind on his hurt and abused body. He felt the separation of his Father, when he said...

***My God, my God, why have you abandoned me...* and did it all for man, for you and for me.**

His Blood freed you from the curse, from poverty, from pain and brokenness. His heart was broken to heal yours, and became sin, so you

don't have to sin. He took the disease so you don't have to be sick.

The Bible says that: *God will wipe every tear in the heart of them, and there will be no more tears and pain, because the former things have passed away.* Jesus heals the brokenhearted to clean their wounds. Let Him heal the pain there inside you through his shed blood, then your uncured pain becomes a blessing in your life. Bitterness and hatred will no longer be part of your life; when you receive the joy of the Lord, the windows of heaven will open over your life and you'll see the light of a new day. Joy is a way of life, and your heart heals with the knowledge of the Word.

Nehemiah 8:10 KJV

... neither be ye sorry; for the joy of the Lord is your strength.

When you are healed of the heart, you regain not only joy, but:

1. You'll become strong in the faith.
2. You'll not be bitter.
3. You'll be happy and your joy will captivate those who surround you.

Although you've walked for many years with a hurting heart, bitter and resentful; Jesus Christ wants to heal it completely. You have to allow the healing power of Jesus to flow and heal your heart and fill it with joy, allowing that joy to be your strength all the time. When someone is bitter they do not have the life of God flowing in their life. A bitter person always complains and sees errors in others.

Christians must have revelation to understand that the church must not be anxious and overwhelmed but must achieve full joy for their children, and everything that the enemy has used for evil, bring it to good.

LESSON 10
BRUISED FOR ALL THE SINS OF THE WORLD

The entire body of Jesus was full of bruises and hematomas. Hematoma is the accumulation of blood caused by internal bleeding, which means rupture of capillaries without releasing blood to the body's surface.

How are they formed? They appear as bumps resulting from blows. All those strikes produced internal and external bruises throughout the body of Jesus. The prophet Isaiah wrote of it many years before it happened: ... *He was bruised for our iniquities.*

Have you ever thought of the kind of blows suffered by Jesus Christ, and the huge hematoma that he had on his shoulder from the weight of the cross? It is thought that the weight that Jesus carried may have been approximately 136 kilos. His exhaustion was obvious, he was arrested the night before and had been completely beaten and flagellated by the whip of Rome.

Isaiah 53:5 KJV

*But he was wounded for our transgressions, **he was bruised for our iniquities:** the chastisement of our peace was upon him; and with his stripes we are healed.*

If there is a bruise on the body it means that it is bleeding internally; now think a bit ... all of his body bleeding, lungs, stomach and liver. Everything in Him was bleeding, however Jesus thought only, *-my blood shed is going to make them suitable in front of my Father.*

His Love Conquered the Iniquity that Separated Us From God

The Iniquity is the essence of evil that wants to drain your spiritual life and dry it up, so that you do not see the truth and God's plan is never established in your life. It is the spiritual force that penetrates into the soul when the person persists in sinning and its evil is never redeemed.

The person itself does not know how to be free or can't; that's why they come out of a situation and return again falling into the same. Only the power of the Holy Blood of Christ breaks the slavery that produces the iniquity.

God wants to set you free, because the Bible says that He paid for your iniquities.

He died to go to the gates of hell to retrieve the keys of life and death, so the curse produced by iniquity would be broken. This force of evil wanted always to destroy mankind so that it would never reach the freedom that comes from the victorious death of Christ on the cross.

The Bible says that the iniquities would pass from the parents to the children unto the third and fourth generation. Which means that iniquity is in mankind, and is passed on through the generations.

Jesus not only was wounded for our transgressions, but came to make changes in man oppressed by the generational iniquity.

It's something like having a bad character, to becomimg a benevolent person. From being completely wicked, to come to love God and seek his holiness.

Jesus was bled internally to make a miracle in your interior.

- Go from being a man addicted, to a healthy man, with new neurons.
- From being a woman with hateful impulses, to being an example, full of goodness.
- From being a bitter person, to change to a happy person.

Thousands of people around the world hear the voice of the Gospel but remain captives in the same way or worse still. What can give you true freedom, is to know the truth; Jesus Christ said: I am the way that takes you to the heavenly Father.

Knowledge, is what comes from God to reveal himself to your life, and when that knowledge comes to your understanding, it's to make you free, because it comes with the truth that sets you free.

When you know the truth of God through his Word, there is no weakness or problem that you don't know how to solve, there will not even be opposition from the enemy that can detain the progress of your relationship with God.

Do not allow any work of evil that can detain you, when you understand in whom you have trusted and who is your provider.

There is a key to receive the blessings of God, it is not only knowing you're saved, but that you're transformed from the old man to a new creature. Being transformed is the result of being free from iniquity.

2 *Corinthians* 5:15, 17 KJV

15 *And that he died for all, that they which live should not henceforth live unto themselves, but unto him which died for them, and rose again…* 17 *Therefore if any man be in Christ, he is a new creature: old things are passed away; behold, all things are become new.*

If you understand the power transferred by God into your life, you are transformed to live for him who died and rose for you. What should be you biggest passion? Christ.

Jesus was bruised for your sins and iniquities, and the Blood of Christ makes you free physically, emotionally and spiritually. You can reclaim the Blood of Jesus so that it can purify you from your sins and iniquity that impulses you to do what many times you do not want to do.

People who have suffered internal bleeding, unseen are the signs on the outside, but inside they are injured and moaning in pain. Many feel lonely, in pain and do not know how to ask for help, as they are internal bruises that nobody sees. Probably, someone has an internal injury, spilling blood that cannot be seen and that no one has seen. When a part of the body is bruised, this area is sensitive and does not want anybody to touch it due to the pain it causes; that's the same feeling a person has that is in pain inside; but Jesus Christ died on the cross and shed precious blood so that they can be free.

2 *Corinthians* 5:21 KJV

For he hath made him to be sin for us, who knew no sin; that we might be made the righteousness of God in him.

Paul transmitted faithfully to the people of Corinth the beautiful truth of Christ, speaking and without losing heart of the real revelation and the redemptive power that hides in the person of Jesus Christ.

He who never sinned and disobeyed, God made him sin, spiritually transformed into a snake; taking the wickedness of humanity so that you

would be justified in Him.

Jesus was bruised to understand what a soul in pain feels. God does not desire the worst situation in your life, on the contrary He desires the best for you. While the spirit of iniquity makes you believe you're not important to God, there is a very big power in all the body of Christ shedding blood; the arteries, the collapsed heart, and everything that scientifically has been investigated in how Jesus died on the cross, which was not a casual fact but the deep love of God to your life.

What is a known truth? It is a rule of life that becomes a way of life in you. A revealed truth known, is a level of behavior; it is a principle that changes you and is something that will always keep you in profound growth with God. When you know the truth at the assembly of God, it makes you have a behavior different from the rest of the people, it makes you change the priorities and understand that there is a principle of God who does not change or stops when you are born or you die. Its principles are revealed truths and are not subjected to human behavior patterns. There is a principle which does not change:

The heaven and earth pass, but God's Word is immutable.

Free From the Spirit of Accusation

One of the things that come to your life when you have understood that the Blood of Christ cleanses you is rest. You learn to rest in the Lord while others run in an uncontrolled form of stress and anguish. When the Holy Spirit takes control of your life and you are free of the accusing mind and of the conscious oppressed by guilt, it is when the Spirit of God brings to your life a state of rest and you can conquer the accuser and doing what God wants you to do.

When the devil arises with an evil accusation, the first thing you have to do is cry out for the sprinkling of the Blood of Christ. The Bible teaches us that we must have faith in his Name and in his Blood to be free of the accusations of the devil. When your life is oppressed by accusing spirits you must depend on the efficacy of the Blood of Christ on your life. Remember, therefore that you can no longer live under condemnation and fear:

Hebrews 10:22 *NLT*

...let us go right into the presence of God with sincere hearts fully trusting him. For our

guilty consciences have been sprinkled with Christ's blood to make us clean, and our bodies have been washed with pure water.

Here are the benefits you receive, when you've been sprinkled with the Blood of Christ:

1. The Blood of Christ redeemed you from sin and darkness.
2. The Blood of Christ is your hedge of protection against the attack from the power of darkness.
3. The Blood of Christ sealed the Covenant between God and man.
4. The Blood of Christ produces a high degree of sanctification.
5. The Blood of Christ cleanses you.
6. The Blood of Christ gives you life in eternity.
7. The Blood of Christ gives you entrance to the Holy of Holies. To a direct relationship with God without reproach and without accusation.

Many people have recognized Jesus as their Lord and Savior but they are unaware of all that the Blood of Jesus has done for them. And not knowing about what it produces over your life weakens your faith in God. I ask you... Why do people live with fear and condemnation? Because they have not understood the power there is in being justified by the Blood of the Lamb.

For example, a man has an unpayable debt and no matter how much he strives to try to pay it off, he knows that even though he dies he will continue owing it because it is a great sum. But suddenly this man, who is employed by a company, one day the owner of the company decides to pay the debt without explaining the details. One day, they call him and tell him: "*look, this is the debt that you have*" and he is given a file with everything he owes; but on the first page there is a paper that has written the following statement: "*cancelled and paid*". However, thinking to yourself, that this man does not read the first page and begins to read the detail of the entire debt saying: "*it is impossible, I cannot pay this*". He thinks at that moment that his fate will be jail because he cannot cancel the debt because he did not see the first page that reads the debt was cancelled and paid in full.

This is a living example that illustrates to you how Satan has trapped the lives of many who he has as slaves and condemned to spiritual debts. The Bible says that "*the wages of sin is death*" the debt that is before God is priceless, it can never be amortized. Therefore, every human being has no way of paying for it. But by accepting Christ as the only Redeemer, He paid for them the debt before the Father.

This is what happens to many Christians at this time; they don't know that their sin has been covered and paid only by having faith in the Blood of Jesus. We must receive this benefit by faith to receive the effect of what this Blood produces. Jesus purchased our lives legally in the cross of Calvary. Peter says, "not by gold or silver but by blood". The Blood of Christ shed on the cross makes you just before the Father, and if it makes you just, He himself cancels your debt. So when the enemy condemns you for your past life, present him with the Act of the New Covenant where it is stated that your sins, and your debt has been cancelled.

1 John 1:7 NLT

...and the blood of Jesus, his Son, cleanses us from all sin.

The sprinkled Blood cleanse you from all sin and this is a continuous work that the Holy Spirit reminds you of every day. You have to understand that the Blood of Christ cleanses you and Satan must flee from you; and this will, not as a result of what you are, but of what you have. Remember that you are full of God's Presence and that makes you to be strengthened and to be victorious, glorious in Jesus Christ. It is important to emphasize this biblical text:

Revelation 12:11 NLT

And they have defeated him by the blood of the Lamb and by their testimony. And they did not love their lives so much that they were afraid to die.

Here we talk about two very important issues:

1. The Blood of the Lamb.
2. The Word of their testimony (this means, that if you believe in the power of the Blood of Christ you testify the victorious power in it). What does God expect of you once you were sprinkled with the Blood of Jesus?
3. That you commit to love him and serve him.
4. That you may live in peace and never doubt.

LESSON 11
THE SPRINKLED BLOOD

Many years ago a hymn was song that said: "*there is power, power, wonder working power (in Jesus who died) in the precious Blood of the Lamb (Jesus)*", but you can see believers today, have little or no understanding of the meaning of the power that is in the blood of Jesus. Often some Christians cry out to that Power, but it is very different to cry out to the blood of Jesus Christ with revelation and knowledge of what implicates the Power of that Blood.

It is true that the blood:

- **Protects at a given time**, such as accident, robbery, sexual assault attack, it is a protection for those who walk in holiness before God.
- **Forgives all your sins, when you go to the throne of Father God** with faith and humility.
- **Makes you free from the oppression of iniquity.**
- **Gives testimony on the earth about the divinity of Christ.**
- **The blood reveals Jesus Christ, and at the same time connects you with the Spirit of truth**

The Word is the living manifestation of the Spirit of truth, it was made flesh and alive in the Son of God and are connected. The Spirit of truth, the Blood and the Word, form the Word of God.

1 John 5:8 KJV

... And there are three that bear witness in earth, the Spirit, and the water, and the blood: and these three agree in one.

The Bible speaks of two forms that it should be poured.

- Spilled.
- Sprinkled.

The majority of believers have knowledge about the Blood that Jesus shed for humanity on the cross of Calvary. Before this happened, the Lord was gathered with his disciples celebrating Passover; He broke bread representing his body, which was going to be crushed and wounded by your sins on the cross and lifted the cup saying: *for this is my blood, which confirms the covenant between God and his people. It is poured out as a sacrifice to forgive the sins of many. Matthew 26:28 (NLT).* **Many only understand the meaning of the blood that was shed on the Cross, and little know what the sprinkled blood means in the Old Testament.**

THE BLOOD SPRINKLED ON THE LINTEL OF THE DOOR

The first biblical reference in this manner of its use is found in **Exodus 12:22**. At that time the angel of death was about to be unleashed in Egypt, and God planned how to protect his people: every family should sacrifice a lamb and keep that blood. **They also were given the order to take a bunch of hyssop, dip it in the blood of that lamb and smear the lintel and the two posts of the door of each house.** When the angel of death passed, and saw the blood smeared on the lintels of the doors, it would go on along and that house would not suffer any harm.

In this biblical story, there are two important points:

- While the blood was being saved in the vessel (although it was spilled), it was not producing any protective effect while not being smeared.
- It was poured, but it had to be applied appropriately.

The Israelites could leave the vessel next to the door of their homes, and say: "*no matter what we do with the blood, just leaving it there, will serve for something*"... think for a moment what would have happened if they left the blood in the vessel and placed it near the door, or on top of a table and they had not obeyed what God told them? **The angel of death would have entered that home and the eldest son should die.**

The order was that the blood had to be t aken out of the vessel and be smeared over the posts so that it served as protection against the angel of death.

The Bible says that everything that happened in the Old Testament, was a shadow of what was to come through the person of Jesus Christ. Each event that Israel lived was a shadow of what Jesus had to do in the prophetic future; this form of blood shed of the lamb, then put on the lintel of the door, was a type and figure of the Blood that Christ, the Lamb of God, poured on the cross.

The Blood of Christ was not wasted it was gathered in a heavenly cup and

the rest of it is to be sprinkled onto the people of God. (Exodus 24:6)

When the Blood of Jesus is sprinkled over your life, you will be under complete protection of all works of darkness.

At the moment that Satan realizes that you've been sprinkled by the Blood of Jesus (just as the posts and lintel of the houses of the Israelites were smeared) in the same way he will have to go on along without being able to damage you.

Every human being that has been sprinkled by the Blood of Jesus, cannot be touched by any demonic spirit. They cannot void the seal of the covenant that has been established through the Blood of Jesus.

So you must understand that the precious Blood is more than forgiving your sins; the Blood of Jesus is alive and available to you 24 hours a day. There is power in the Blood sprinkled on your life since it is the blood of the Covenant.

***Exodus 24:8* KJV**

And Moses took the blood, and sprinkled it on the people, and said, Behold the blood of the covenant, which the Lord hath made with you concerning all these words.

I encourage you to read Exodus 24 at home, where it speaks of the sprinkling of the Blood and you can study in depth this topic. God commands to summon his servants such as: Moses, Aaron, Nadab, and Abihu with seventy elders. The remaining people were further away from the mount. Moses takes the blood of the "peace offering", placed half in bowls, and with the other half sprinkled it over the people who make a covenant with God to fulfil the words of the law that are written in the tablets of God. And he said on behalf of YHVH God: "*I will be your God and you shall be my people*"; after that Moses established the law to Israel, they answered, "*we understand and we will obey*"; the people agreed to enter into **covenant with God**.

***Hebrews 9:19* NLT**

For after Moses had read each of God's commandments to all the people, he took the blood of calves and goats, along with water, and sprinkled both the book of God's law and all the people, using hyssop branches and scarlet wool.

The Blood Sprinkled over the 12 Columns

Then Moses sprinkled the twelve columns of the tabernacle, which represent the twelve tribes of Israel, and finally sprinkled the people with the blood, thus sealing the people with God. To sprinkle with the blood was granting the Israelites a full assurance of access and communion with God. In this biblical passage it does not refer to forgiveness, or remission of sins, but rather communion and establishment **of a Covenant that God had to do with Israel and the people with God.**

The Blood gives us forgiveness, sanctifies us to be part of their presence, the leaders and elders of Israel, could see him and gaze in his beauty and enjoy the Presence of God, gazing sheltered under the security that is in it.

Today we are in a New Covenant with Jesus Christ, superior to the Old Covenant. When his Blood is sprinkled over each man and woman it is with the purpose that each have communion and direct access to the Presence of God. You'll not only have communion but you will be purified with the sprinkling of the blood.

Don't have the slightest doubt of getting close to the throne of the Father through the blood that covers you, only make a covenant with God of faithfulness and to keep his written Word.

The Blood Sprinkled Over the Mercy Seat

One of the most important sprinkling of blood that was carried out, was that of the **atonement for sins,** which means "the reconciliation with God".

The purpose of this act was to erase the sins of the people and to be accountable with God. The priest was to take a censer full of coals of fire from the altar, and there was also blood from the sacrificed animal, in the Holy of Holies within the Tabernacle. In the Holy of Holies there was an ark, with a golden lid with two cherubim, it was as if God would sit on it and represented his very presence. The mercy seat had two golden cherubim, one on each side with its wings extended covering it. The priest sprinkled the blood seven times on the mercy seat, and when this was happening, the forgiveness of all sins were covered by this prophetic act. There were two important things in them, not only that the priest did as God had specified him to do, but that the major signal was that the priest came out alive.

The Only High Priest that exists, is at the right of the Father, interceding for each of us.

He carries out this work 365 days a year, and will continue to be our High Priest for eternity (Hebrews 6:20). Jesus took his own Blood, and took it to the mercy seat of the presence, not in a place on earth, but in heaven, where the real Holy of Holies is and presented it to the Father for the remission of all the sins of all believers for ever and ever. (Hebrews 9:12, 14)

The Blood of Jesus is available for every sinner who wants to repent and wishes to enter in the presence of the Father. That Blood will sprinkle him for forgiveness, sanctification, communication and will give him direct access to the Presence of God.

Jesus sprinkled his blood on us, when by faith we accept his work finished on the cross of Calvary. Perhaps this is not a physical sprinkling, rather it is a spiritual transaction where He sprinkled his Blood on our life, in response to our faith placed in Him. And until it is not believed in the power of his sacrifice on Calvary and its Salvation is not accepted in the heart, the Blood of Jesus will not produce anything in our soul.

The Bible says that we have to have faith in his Name, but we also need to have faith in his Blood.

When Moses sprinkled the blood of the Lamb on the Israelites that had failed, they did not doubt for a moment that they had been forgiven, because it was the shed blood of an animal on the altar of the burnt offering. If they understood that dimension of the power of the blood of an animal, much more a Christian must have conviction of what the Blood of Christ sprinkled over their lives mean.

Martin Luther said: "it is a blasphemy to take the sins which were place upon Jesus Christ and have it placed upon us again". When you know that the Blood of Christ clean your sins, but don't believe it, this disbelief takes you to upload them again and place them on your life.

When you proclaim the victory of the blood of Christ, and you praise with your heart for the promise of this great redemption that the Lord made in your life, you begin to be lifted in strength, and you'll begin to be blessed and impacted by the presence of the Lord.

Romans 5:11 *NLT*

So now we can rejoice in our wonderful new relationship with God because our Lord Jesus Christ has made us friends of God.

LESSON 12

WHY IS THE BLOOD OF JESUS PRECIOUS?

The Apostle Peter speaks of several things that are beautiful, when mentioning this qualifier he refers to what has to do with the quality of excellence, exquisite, fine and worthy of estimation and appreciation, something of great value or of a high cost.

1 Peter 1:18-20 *NLT*

19 *It was the precious blood of Christ, the sinless, spotless Lamb of God...*

In all of Scriptures when mentioning the blood of Jesus Christ there is used a real and genuine qualifier which is: "precious" and is an absolute truth, only His blood is recognized as such.

In verse seven of the same chapter it mentions that:

1. **Faith is much more precious** than gold.
2. **The Pearl of great value and precious** (Matthew 13:46)
3. Peter also qualifies **as precious the Blood of Christ.**
4. In chapter two, verse four of the same book speaks of **the living gemstone**, which represents the foundation of the building that is Christ, as precious and there in verse seven, says that,
5. **Christ is precious** to believers.

The word "**precious**" in Greek is /*timios*/ meaning: honorable, dear, something of great value. And the four characteristics refer to Christ. **Have you ever asked yourself why that blood is so precious?** Because it is the only blood that has effectiveness in the spiritual world and is efficient to erase the sins before God the Father.

Only the Blood of the Lamb of God has the power to save; the sacrifice of Jesus on the cross was sufficient so that men and women were forgiven and washed of their sins.

While Jesus was developing his ministry on earth, Satan the old deceiver watched what He was doing. The people:

- they were freed from oppression and
- of illnesses;
- the blind and the deaf were healed,
- the lame were walking,
- the lepers were cleansed,
- the dead resurrected

While Jesus was on earth he was destroying the works of evil that oppressed people. In a progressive way He was manifesting the power he had to submit all under the Presence of God.

Satan was upset and enraged against Jesus Christ, which is why he planned to destroy and kill him on the cross. He planted the evil in the heart of those who should have accepted him; he sowed hatred in those who should have loved him, and it was for this reason that they preferred to see him crucified than doing good! If he had known what would happen after his death, he had never incited to crucify him; because it is precisely that precious Blood shed on the cross that removed the dominion that Satan had on men and women.

Satan would have never wanted Jesus to pour out his Blood, because he did not understand that by dying on the cross, Jesus was going to destroy the dominion of sin on human beings.

Observe this example: people are not clean just by knowing there exists an element of cleansing called soap, they need to take it in their hands and use it to remove dirt from the body. That is what it means to discern the Blood of Jesus, when taken in the Lord's Supper. Nothing will serve you to talk about the Blood of Jesus, his power and authority if you don't apply it to your life. If you do not know that it has the authority to wash away sins; you'll still be carrying them, because you ignore the genuine power that exists therein for redemption.

It is not only to know about the Blood of Christ and know about its existence, but understand that it is different from any other blood that can be compared. Your blood is common, but the Blood of Jesus is Holy!

WHY WAS THE BLOOD OF JESUS HOLY?

In the moment of our conception, all of us have inherited characteristics, group and blood factor. Usually a blood test allows to determine family kinship through DNA testing.

It is scientifically proven that 15 types of blood exist, in addition to specific groups that are detected in some isolated families, and others that are in different persons. According to medicine, a blood system can include one or several antigens of factors of blood types.

It is verified that the RH of a mother can be positive and that her child may be negative. The mother's blood nourishes the fetus through the placenta, which in turn prevents the mother's blood entrance into the blood veins of the baby. That is to say, the blood of the woman who is pregnant feeds the placenta, but the child has his own blood. However, it should be noted that with Jesus there appeared a situation different from that of any human being.

He did not have an earthly father, then it would not be possible to group his Blood because it was unique; the Precious and Holy Blood was independent of any genetic heritage.

God inspired the evangelist Luke, who was a doctor, to write about it, so that mankind when reading the Bible understood the details that Mary was a witness to. She was able to speak without shame, with a doctor like him, and that is why we read what happened:

Luke 1:34-35 *NLT*

34 Mary asked the angel, "But how can this happen? I am a virgin." 35 The angel replied,
"The Holy Spirit will come upon you, and the power of the Most High will overshadow
you. So the baby to be born will be holy, and he will be called the Son of God.

Mary and Joseph were engaged, but had not yet had an intimate relationship. Until that moment, she was a virgin woman. What in her womb had been conceived, was a great miracle of the Almighty Heavenly Father; therefore, the body of Jesus had not inherited anything of Joseph or his ancestors. With respect to the blood of Maria, a woman can give birth to a child that is incompatible with her own blood type. For example, the baby develops his own blood in his mother's womb and can even be a type opposite to his own mother, as we have said.

The secret of the power of the Blood of Jesus is that it was the Blood of the Only Begotten of the Father. Every human blood is contaminated by sin, but only the Blood of Jesus was without genetic contamination of sin.

In addition to Jesus, there was a man whose blood was not received by genetic means. It was the first time that a man was receiving blood through the divine.

Adam was created by God, the Lord blew life in him. What was the blood that ran through the veins of Adam? Who put that blood in him? Adam had no mother, nor was conceived. He was the first man who is mentioned as a son of God according to his ancestry. In other words, Adam was a special creation without human ancestor. Jesus is called in the Bible the last Adam, the latter, which previously there was only one.

Luke 3:38 *NLT*

Kenan was the son of Enosh. Enosh was the son of Seth. Seth was the son of Adam. Adam was the son of God.

The body of Jesus as the body of Adam, was specially prepared as the Bible says:

Hebrews 10:5-7, 15-17 *NLT*

5 That is why, when Christ came into the world, he said to God, "You did not want animal sacrifices or sin offerings. But you have given me a body to offer. 6 You were not pleased with burnt offerings or other offerings for sin. 7 Then I said, 'Look, I have come to do your will, O God – as is written about me in the Scriptures.'"
15 And the Holy Spirit also testifies that this is so. For he says, 16 "This is the new covenant I will make with my people on that day, says the Lord: I will put my laws in their hearts, and I will write them on their minds." 17 Then he says, "I will never again remember their sins and lawless deeds."

God made that Mary conceive a son, without going through the normal biological needs. And this was possible, because there is nothing impossible for God. However, there is a big difference between the first Adam and the last Adam.

The first man was made of the earth, and the second man was made from heaven.

The contamination of Adam by sin, entered, contaminated and damaged his blood, and ran through the veins of all of us. But for the reasons mentioned before, that did not circulated through the Blood of Jesus, that's why his Blood is Holy. The birth of Jesus was the great miracle of the Father because it happened differently from any human.

THE BLOOD OF JESUS IS FROM GOD

The Bible speaks of the Precious Blood of Jesus but also says that the blood of Jesus is, the Blood of God.

Acts 20:28 *NLT*

So guard yourselves and God's people. Feed and shepherd God's flock—his church, ***purchased with his own blood—over which the Holy Spirit*** *has appointed you as elders.*

Here it tells us that the Church was bought with the precious blood of Jesus, understanding that God is Spirit, that no flesh or blood; the answer is simple, the Word became man, the Word was made flesh and dwelt among us, and we saw his glory as the only Begotten of the Father. In the womb of Mary, the deity and humanity were unified. For this reason we say that the Blood of Jesus is the Blood of God, is Divine, Holy and Precious.

THE BLOOD OF CHRIST IS EFFECTIVE

The Blood of the Almighty is fully effective from the legal point of view. An individual can shed his blood and give his life in place of others, but the Blood of Jesus has no limitation to anyone. **Here intervened the grace and mercy of God.** The Blood of the Son of God has the sufficient grace, to cover all the sin of anyone who repents and believes in Him. God demonstrated the power of the blood, when Israel came out of Egypt. The Israelites had to sacrifice and eat the Passover lamb. The Bible says that if a family was very small, it could share the lamb with another family.

Exodus 12:4 *NLT*

If a family is too small to eat a whole animal, let them share with another family in the neighborhood. Divide the animal according to the size of each family and how much they can eat.

This is a way of understanding what Jesus did; He is the Lamb of God that is too large for a single family. He must be for all the families in your neighborhood, your town, your nation. Jesus Christ is the true atonement for the sins of all who believe in Him. John saw an apocalyptic revelation, which had a great multitude, which no one could count; they had washed their clothes and made white in the Blood of the Lamb:

Revelation 7:9 NLT

After this I saw a vast crowd, too great to count, from every nation and tribe and people and language, standing in front of the throne and before the Lamb. They were clothed in white robes and held palm branches in their hands.

THE BLOOD OF CHRIST ALSO SPEAKS

Hebrews 12:24 NLT

You have come to Jesus, the one who mediates the new covenant between God and people, and to the sprinkled blood, which speaks of forgiveness instead of crying out for vengeance like the blood of Abel.

Here we are told that the Blood of Jesus speaks better than that of Abel.

Genesis 4:10-11 NLT

10 *But the Lord said, "What have you done? Listen! Your brother's blood cries out to me from the ground!* 11 *Now you are cursed and banished from the ground, which has swallowed your brother's blood.*

The blood of Abel spilled on the ground what was it denouncing? Death, murder and demanded revenge.

The Blood of Christ also stained the earth as did the blood of Abel, but with a big difference, the Blood of Jesus was talking about life, not death. The blood of Abel demanded revenge, but the Blood of Christ offered forgiveness to all who approached Him.

Charles Wesley spoke about the bleeding wounds in the body of Jesus and said something very true: *"without that Blood, there would be no life in the human being."*

Cain was punished for the death of his brother Abel, but nobody received punishment for the death of Christ on Calvary. Christ suffered death for you, and because of that you cannot stay quiet, and you should tell all what Christ did for you and for them.

Calvary did not give origin to revenge, nor to hatred, nor to retaliation; Calvary is known as mercy to the sinner.

When Jesus shed his blood on the cross, he had to have sprayed the Roman soldiers who had crucified him, and their hands were stained with the death of Christ; however, Luke 23:34 tells that Jesus said: *"Father, forgive them, for they don't know what they are doing."* There is no forgiveness of sins if there is no spilling of Blood. This is only by the Blood of Jesus Christ, which is a Blood that speaks and has eternal life.

The Important thing is to appropriate the divine forgiveness, because through the Blood of Jesus all your sins of yesterday, today, and forever will be forgiven.

After that the Blood of Jesus stained ground, that same Blood cleaned you.

The flood killed all sinners, Noah and his family were saved, but when he came out of the ark he made a Blood sacrifice. The flood water did not wash the sin, only the Blood of Christ is powerful to do so.

His Blood pays for everything, for by it we have been re-acquired, and rescued for God the Father.

Since the man sold his soul when covenanting with Satan selling himself to sin, falling to the lowest. That is why he needed someone to pay for his rescue, since he was in the showcase of the slaves. Jesus paid the ransom, not with silver coins or of gold but with a higher price that is his blood.

That is why we should love the blood because it was the price to pay for my rescue. The price of your salvation was too expensive, and there was no human currency that could attain the value to buy it.

The Blood of Jesus Gives Life and is Eternal

Jesus has given you a secure salvation and it is the mark of his precious blood on you, that no one can remove, not even separate you from the arms of your Savior. Satan cannot kidnap your soul when you've made a covenant of holiness with Christ. Over your life is the seal of the blood as an eternal sign. This signal is permanent, and is weather-proof.

The Blood of Jesus does not give you license to sin, on the contrary God gave it to you for salvation.

If you do not have assurance of your salvation and don't know if you're clean of your sins you can do it today, recognizing Christ as your Savior. **Tell him right now and say this prayer in front of His Presence.**

"Lord, I you need. Father that is in heaven and in every place through Your Spirit, I humble myself in front of Your Presence in the mighty Name of Jesus, and put in front of you, all of my mistakes, my failures, my sins, problems and addictions that I have not been able to remove by myself. God and eternal Father, I ask you in the Name of Jesus to wash me with the Precious Blood of Jesus, which He shed at Calvary. Break every tie and covenant with Satan, let it be broken and shattered in my life, and in my family. Mark me internally and externally with Your Precious Blood and I'll be yours forever in spirit, soul and body, now and for eternity. Lord Jesus, I put my faith, my trust in you. I believe that you are the Son of the living God, and I believe with all my heart what at this moment I am confessing with my mouth. You are my Savior, my God. I believe that I was born again and am a child of the Most High God and proclaim it in the Name of Jesus", Amen.

LESSON 13

ATONEMENT BY HIS BLOOD

Unfortunately, one of the issues that people understand little is about the effect and characteristics of the atonement. The Bible mentions several terms in relation to the reconciliation of man with God where the following words are used: **atonement, redemption and propitiation**.

Each one of these words guard within themselves the mystery of God, hidden in favor of human beings. What is its effectiveness? What sense has for the man the atoning work of Christ and what does it produce in him? To have knowledge about this topic, we invite you to read the following text in the Bible in Hebrews 9:11-28.

Evidently the effect that produces the atonement in a life, as it is revealed in the 11th chapter of Hebrews is:

1. FORGIVENESS OF TRANSGRESSIONS:

   Jesus Christ paid the debt that you would have never been able to pay. In his atoning work there was a radical payment, in favor of your life.

2. REDEMPTION:

   God ensured that you were free through the remission of sins. When the Bible speaks of remit; meaning: remove, root out, to forgive. The Blood of Jesus Christ was effective to delete all kinds of sin. When you recognize Jesus Christ as your personal Savior, it does not mean that you entered into an ideology or a new philosophy; when you are born again and recognize Jesus Christ as your Lord and Savior within you has begun a new life and all your sins of the past, will never be remembered by God, as if He would bring them back to memory, it would have been in vain the sacrifice of Christ on the cross.

   The Bible speaks of three dimensions that oppress the human being, and are inside of what transgression means: sin, rebellion and iniquity. Of each one of them, the sacrifice of Christ made expiation. The first thing to discern when speaking of atonement is of a price that has been paid for you. A price that never the federal reserve of a country could have paid. The only one who redeemed you is called Jesus Christ, for he died in your place. Remember that the wages of sin is death, but Jesus occupied your place, he was given by the Father to be your substitute provision, and died so that you have life in abundance. That is why the Bible says that you were free of the transgressions.

3. FREEDOM FROM SIN:

Through the atonement, the believer not only is free of their past sins, but from the power of sin in the present and future according to what the Apostle Paul mentioned in:

Romans 6:1-2 NLT

Well then, should we keep on sinning so that God can show us more and more of his wonderful grace? 2 Of course not! Since we have died to sin, how can we continue to live in it?

Paul explains that even the thought of living a sinful life should make you feel bad. He also says, that who has Christ as their Lord and Savior is definitely separated in virtue of their faith and trust in the author and finisher of his life. Faith in Jesus is a living faith, because you have believed in Him as "*the one who conquered death and lives forever*". The risen Savior has given as a result the crucifixion of your sinful nature.

The man and the woman who believes with all their heart that Christ died for the sins, have a firm faith inside them. The cross means death and downfall of sin in your life forever. The tempter, father of lies and god of this age, continually harassed man and attacks the human nature that is weak and fragile. Sin cannot control you and touch your life to do what he wants, because you are not under the law but in the grace, covered by the love that He has for you and made it truthful through his sacrifice.

Romans 6:14 NLT

Sin is no longer your master, for you no longer live under the requirements of the law. Instead, you live under the freedom of God's grace.

The law determines that the sinner must do something to be free of that guilt, but for as more as he does he'll never cancel that debt, and in not doing so, the human being would remain forever under the dominion of sin. But on the other hand the grace revealed through Jesus has been revealed, and tells you that something has been done for the sinner, in a miraculous and powerful way. To that it is called the perfect and finished work on the cross of Calvary.

FAITH ALIVE AND POWERFUL

In what has to do with the faith alive and powerful, you have an ally that is called the divine paracleto who is the person of the Holy Spirit, who is responsible of revealing Jesus to you in your life. Without Him, no one can understand the mystery of the cross, the atonement and redemption, unless it is revealed by Him. Without God's Holy Spirit it is difficult to understand the Father's love, the perfect work of the cross and the effective power of the shed blood.

When the Holy Spirit comes and makes shadow in your life, He will dwell within you, and what previously was not understood about the mystery of the cross will now be understandable, and will also help you to believe that if you have a living faith, you will crush all sinful thoughts that come into your life.

The Holy Spirit tells you: "*you can do it, that's why Jesus resurrected so that you don't have death, you can overcome, because He died for you and was your substitute so you can be a conqueror*".

The Holy Spirit helps you to pray, and gives you the freedom you now have in Jesus. Truly Christ died to remove the obstacle of sin, so that his Spirit comes to dwell in your life.

The believer who lives every day by the cross, will receive an experience of:

1. **CLEANLINESS**:

   The believer who cleanses every day their sins with the Blood of Christ, is because they have understood the meaning of that sacrifice. In this type of believer, there is evident a spiritual cleanliness, which will lead them to seek God continually.

2. **SPIRITUAL REVIVAL:**

   A believer experiences revival when he loves the search and the holiness of God. This is a believer who said: No to sin! The revival comes as a result of a spiritual quest of cleanliness and brings life in abundance. (Titus 3:5-7). When you allow the Holy Spirit to work in you, and make you obedient to God, you adapt to the new life in Christ, and the Holy Spirit will give you eternal life and abundantly.

3. FREE FROM DEATH:

Death has a physical and spiritual meaning. When the Bible speaks to you of spiritual death it refers to the penalty assigned by God to human sin. Who dies without Christ, weighs upon him a sentence of physical death without hope of resurrection to new life, and also carries the spiritual sentence of being separated from the Presence of God. Sin is what assigns this sentence.

When a person dies and never reconciled with God in life, will remain separated from God in the other world forever. They will be called to experience eternal separation which follows and is known as the second death. The declaration that God made Adam, enclosed all the criminal consequences arising from sin in the human being, such as separation from God, restlessness, anxiety, desiring evil, physical weakness, reaching physical death, and all kinds of consequences that brings this death.

But the Bible says when Christ died for our sins, he submitted not only to the physical death, but what weighed on him like an agonizing cup, was the consequence of death for the punishment of sin. Jesus was the only one able to humble himself to the sufferings of death so that by the grace of God he might taste death for every human being and in virtue to his divine nature, had to take our human likeness, in this way he could perform this task on behalf of the Father. Perhaps you don't understand how this happened, because it is evident that this is the deepest mystery of the divinity of God: the mystery of the cross.

This is not only the deepest mystery, but the most filled with love that the Father could express toward human beings. At this time, many kill people to establish a religious system. But God the Father who was revealed through the person of Jesus, was not a God of death or mass killings, but the God who was the giver of life, by his voluntary death. Many religions kill, telling people that if they do not convert to them they will be killed and beheaded; Jesus only says: "*come to me, all of you who are weary and carry heavy burdens, and I will give you rest, because he who believes in me although is dead will live*".

No sensible person will be deprived of the benefits of electricity, simply because you don't understand how this works. Likewise, you have to believe what the Word says and the Holy Spirit each time will be revealing the divine purposes of God over your life. No one needs to be deprived of the benefits of the cross simply because you cannot reason in regards to it.

Death is the penalty of sin, but Christ came to give himself for your sins. What did he do? Died for them. The meaning of death, is the dark, separation from God, and this explains the desperate cry of Jesus:

***Matthew 27:46** NLT*

"Eli, Eli, lema sabachthani?" which means "My God, my God, why have you abandoned me?"

Those who were there, they thought Jesus was calling Elijah. But aren't these words perhaps those of a martyr, dying? Is it not perhaps the biggest compassion of the Father for humanity?

Jesus felt the divine separation from the Father; this act meant that He was charged with sin. Have you thought about how Jesus felt on the cross, when He felt the deepest shadow of death, ending his life, being He the giver of life? How would Jesus feel experiencing this act of death in his body without sin?

Religions do not have a God of love, of mercy and of compassion. There are some who deeply love death, but there are others who deeply love life. Jesus felt in all his being that death was finishing him when He himself was the giver of life.

***John 14:8-12** NLT*

8 Philip said, "Lord, show us the Father, and we will be satisfied." 9 Jesus replied, "Have I
been with you all this time, Philip, and yet you still don't know who I am? Anyone who
has seen me has seen the Father! So why are you asking me to show him to you? 10 Don't
you believe that I am in the Father and the Father is in me? The words I speak are not my
own, but my Father who lives in me does his work through me. 11 Just believe that I am in
the Father and the Father is in me. Or at least believe because of the work you have seen
me do. 12 "I tell you the truth, anyone who believes in me will do the same works I have
done, and even greater works, because I am going to be with the Father.

When it was presented to John, he said: "This is the message from the one who is the First and the Last, who was dead but is now alive." (Revelation 2:8)

Although it is true, that those who believe in Him, will perhaps have to suffer, as the Christian brothers in the Middle East are suffering physical punishment; in them the stigma of eternal death has been removed to make way for the life. And it becomes the gate of eternal life. A broader life, and in that sense is confirmed what He said:

John 11:26 NLT

"Everyone who lives in me and believes in me will never ever die."

Jesus paid the price so you don't have to bear the burden of pain, grief, illness, or captivity, I want to remind you that He paid the price to make you free. All those that need to be free and healthy in his soul, body and spirit, believe in this Word that the Lord will minister to you wherever you are. All spirit of disease or oppression has to go in the Name of Jesus. Wherever there is a need, receive the touch from the Lord because only He can cancel the price of sin on the cross of Calvary so you can be free completely and so that the grace of the Almighty God, radiates in your life forever.

If you believe with all your heart and have faith in the effectiveness of the shed and sprinkled blood, I invite you to say this firm prayer:

Padre en el Nombre de Jesús gracias porque Tu Palabra nunca vuelve atrás vacía sino que se afirma en sí misma, y se hace manifiesta en cada vida de una forma clara y poderosa.

Father in the Name of Jesus thank you because your Word never returns back empty but asserts itself, and is made manifest in each life in a clear and powerful way. In the Name of Jesus of Nazareth, help me understand everything that I have read in this book, the dimension, the effect, the power, the authority and the revelation that there is in the Blood that one day Jesus shed on the cross, and meanwhile allow those of us who are part of Your people to approach you confidently, in front of the Throne of your Grace, seeing how the Blood of Jesus Christ is sprinkled in a permanent way on those who receive him as the only Savior of their lives, being accepted to enter in a dependency of trust, in the power of his Name. I confess that your redeemed rise in levels of trust and confidence, because we are confident in who we believed. You are the only one that took away sin forever, and that has been established as the great High Priest between God and man, being the Only One who can advocate for us on the Throne of your Glory. Thank you God for your love and mercy that are unfathomable, in the name of Jesus Christ.

Amen.

LESSON 14

THE POWER OF REGENERATION

God has different ways of operating in the life of every human being. He began initiating a process even if the enemy tries to hinder it or prevent it. God starts and creates, this can be called the beginning of something, and that was what He did with man, although at some point the process was interrupted by the consequence of sin and disobedience, an orchestrated plan that the devil threw in the garden of Eden; but in the midst of all this God established a prophetic Word, in which the future manifestation of the miracle of redemption had been implied in itself. The fulfillment of this would allow for a new beginning and a fulfilment of God's great promise of redemption.

Matthew 19:28 *NLT*

Jesus replied, "I assure you that when the world is made new and the Son of Man sits upon his glorious throne, you who have been my followers will also sit on twelve thrones, judging the twelve tribes of Israel.

Ephesians 4:23-24 *NLT*

[23] *Instead, let the Spirit renew your thoughts and attitudes.* [24] *Put on your new nature, created to be like God – truly righteous and holy.*

What you need to do then is take advantage of this new beginning that God allows in your life with the purpose to be justified by faith and have peace with God and then receive the miracle of the regeneration that you need in your life. As a result, this will allow you to reflect the original plan of God in your life, because in this regeneration you have the activation of the secret of God whereby it ministers new spiritual life; in other words: you are born again. Regeneration, then, is a total work of God from beginning to end in your life; not through any human will, but by the will of God.

THE REGENERATION

The word regeneration is translated from the Greek word /*palingenesis* /, which in turn has its roots in /*palin* /which means new and *Genesis* which means creation. This has to do with the act of God by which He gives eternal life, spiritual life, divine life and a new nature. **It is the regeneration of a new birth.** The only way that a person can have eternal life is through placing their faith in Jesus, since eternal life is a gift from God, it is not something that one can win; man by his fallen nature, seeks substitutes to get to heaven, mostly relying on their good works rather than in the perfect sacrifice of Jesus. But what God says is:

Romans 3:23 *KJV*

For all have sinned, and come short of the glory of God…

It is important to understand that all have sinned, and because of sin then man is separated from God and subject to eternal damnation.

Romans 6:23 *RVR60*

For the wages of sin is death; but the gift of God is eternal life through Jesus Christ our Lord.

That death means eternal damnation in hell; but immediately God gives us the solution, which is Christ. Man has to recognize that the only one who can forgive sin and give salvation to the soul is the Lord Jesus, and only when he/she repents before the Lord is forgiveness obtained. When a person receives Jesus as his only and sufficient personal Savior he has a new birth.

John 3:3 *NLT*

Jesus replied, "I tell you the truth, unless you are born again, you cannot see the Kingdom of God."

Here Jesus was talking to Nicodemus, who was a religious man, a man who was an interpreter of the law, a Pharisee: "Nicodemus, you cannot enter the Kingdom of heaven if you're not born again." *"What do you mean?" exclaimed Nicodemus. "How can an old man go back into his mother's womb and be born again?"* ***John 3:4***

Jesus told Nicodemus that he had to be born again, the Greek word used here is */anodsen/* which means "from above". Nicodemus could not think otherwise than in a physical birth, because he didn't have the spiritual capacity to understand what Jesus was referring to. Eternal life is a gift from God, it is divine grace, and the question is: **When does eternal life begin?**

Eternal life begins at the moment of receiving Jesus as personal Savior. It is God giving eternal life to the saved sinner, through Jesus Christ, and this is the reason why the saved must live for the eternal, not for the temporary thing, nor the passing thing.

2 Corinthians 4:18 KJV

While we look not at the things which are seen, but at the things which are not seen: for the things which are seen are temporal; but the things which are not seen are eternal.

This is the reason why many do not invest in the eternal. Those who are saved must live for the eternal. There are three things that are eternal: God, the Word of God and he who believes in Jesus Christ and has been regenerated.

2 Peter 1:4 NLT

And because of his glory and excellence, he has given us great and precious promises. These are the promises that enable you to share his divine nature and escape the world's corruption caused by human desires.

You can be part of the divine nature. What does this mean? That now you're a child of God. Now you can live the Christian life because you have a divine nature, the nature of God and you can do the things that please God.

James 1:18 NLT

He chose to give birth to us by giving us his true word. And we, out of all creation, became his prized possession.

Born biologically and physically is something that happened to you, but when speaking of regeneration, this is referring to the opportunity that God gives you in your life to connect with eternity, you are therefore identifying yourself with what you'll be in eternity.

1 Peter 1:3 NLT

All praise to God, the Father of our Lord Jesus Christ. It is by his great mercy that we have been born again, because God raised Jesus Christ from the dead...

At the crucifixion, Jesus annulled the code of death, but with his resurrection, activated the code of life so you can be under his wings and trusting that in Him you have the regeneration that was much needed to have eternal v life and immortality.

Colossians 2:13 NLT

You were dead because of your sins and because your sinful nature was not yet cut away. Then God made you alive with Christ, for he forgave all our sins.

What the Father did then is that with the death of Jesus on the cross of Calvary, opened a door for everyone who believes in Him so that they're not lost but have eternal life. Therefore, you need to cast all that you've done contrary to God and His Word, to the bottom of the sea.

This happens when you understand the "restart" that you need in your life. This comes to deliver you from the oppressive hands of the enemy, since what he is doing is making humanity believe that you can play God by means of genetic manipulation, believing that they can achieve a regeneration which is completely false.

This is the reason why humankind moves increasingly more and more further from God because what everyone needs is the restart of God and not that of the devil, through the manipulation of DNA, he does not know with exact precision what that wonderful staircase snail which contains chromosomes with detailed information of each human being is made of; only Christ can reprogram that through the shedding of his blood, giving beginning to the originality of the permanent life. That is why God does not need to do experiments with humans to "improve" them, the Creator already knows everything and can change what He desires at will as He wants.

2 Corinthians 5:17 *NLT*

This means that anyone who belongs to Christ has become a new person. The old life is gone; a new life has begun!

When someone has been regenerated, they have experienced the rebirth, it's as if they were starting again without any contamination, it's as if the DNA was being newly placed again without someone having altered it because what you'll find in Christ is life, a life that cannot can be minimized, on the contrary, when you obey His Word it's empowered and you become a vessel that God will use for blessing all those who surround you.

John 6:65 *NLT*

Then he said, "That is why I said that people can't come to me unless the Father gives them to me."

God has had so much mercy of your life that it has made you surrender completely at the feet of Christ. It is not because of your intellect and that's why today you are before Him; what has happened is that you've been in the heart of the Father and He considered you to be delivered into the hands of your Lord Jesus Christ and that you had the opportunity of being regenerated in your DNA and all of your genetic information. This is what happens when a man or woman responds to the divine calling, the Word of God imparts new spiritual life, there, where man by nature, is spiritually dead.

1 Peter 1:23 NLT

For you have been born again, but not to a life that will quickly end. Your new life will last forever because it comes from the eternal, living word of God.

The power regenerator of the Word of God: exactly equal to how you owe your natural existence to the spoken word of the Creator and the breath of life that blew into you, so also your new birth is due to the activation of the power of the Holy Spirit and the Word of God. The intention of God in regards to you being created is fully complied only when your spirit is vivified in his presence. Just as the sin has produced spiritual death.

Ephesians 2:1-3 NLT

1 Once you were dead because of your disobedience and your many sins. 2 You used to
live in sin, just like the rest of the world, obeying the devil – the commander of the powers
in the unseen world. He is the spirit at work in the hearts of those who refuse to obey God.
3 All of us used to live that way, following the passionate desires and inclinations of our
sinful nature. By our very nature we were subject to God's anger, just like everyone else.

Salvation in Jesus Christ has provided the spiritual life. God has made us to be born again by the power of the Holy Spirit.

Titus 3:5 NLT

He saved us, not because of the righteous things we had done, but because of his mercy. He washed away our sins, giving us a new birth and new life through the Holy Spirit.

In Greek meaning; "*he saved us through the washing of the regeneration and renewing of the Holy Spirit*" and it has also made you a member of the new creation of God. The power of the Word of God in the Holy Scriptures is manifested above all things therein: gives spiritual life to all who receive its truth.

James 1:18 NLT

He chose to give birth to us by giving us his true word. And we, out of all creation, became his prized possession.

You get to be a kind of first fruits of his creatures, this refers to the fact that "the word of truth" is the means by which He gave you a new life, emphasizing that God has made it so, as an expression of His own will. The will of God to save you has been effectively expressed in his Word, if you believe it with all your heart, the new beginning of life has come to you.

Through the resurrection of Jesus Christ, the DNA that was disrupted by the death that came to mankind through sin committed by Adam now is restored to immortality.

John 11:25-26 NLT

[25] *Jesus told her, "I am the resurrection and the life. Anyone who believes in me will live,*
even after dying. [26] *Everyone who lives in me and believes in me will never ever die…*

So, do not worry about what is to come in this earthly life, rather place your eyes on things above where eternal life is, with the confidence that you will live and rule with Him forever. May God bless you richly, now and forever. Amen.

EPILOGUE

On having finished this topic and having read this important article written by a doctor experienced in intensive care, I have believed suitable to share it with every reader of this book.

PATHOPHYSIOLOGY OF THE DEATH OF JESUS CHRIST

Rubén Darío Camargo R.
Internal Medicine - Intensive Care

HE IS A MAN AND A THIRST

Today, based on the knowledge of the pathophysiology of the traumatized patient, it is possible to go so far as to deduce physiological changes endured by Jesus Christ during his passion and death. The Biblical accounts of the crucifixion described through the Gospels and scientific documentation on this matter, describe that he endured and suffered the cruelest of punishments. The most inhuman and ruthless of the treatment that a human being can receive. Archaeological discoveries related to the Roman practices of the crucifixion provide valuable information that gives true historical strength to the figure of Jesus, and his real presence in the history of the man. Historically this event begins during the celebration of the Jewish Passover. The last supper took place on Thursday 6 April (Nisan 13). The crucifixion took place on 7 April (Nisan 14).

GARDEN OF OLIVES (GETHSEMANE)

The sacred writers describe the prayer of Gethsemane with energetic expressions. As lived by Jesus before being taken as a prisoner, they recount it as a mixture of unspeakable sadness, of fright, of tedium and of weakness. This expresses a moral shame that has reached the highest degree of its intensity. It was such a degree of moral suffering, which presented like a manifestation of somatic, physical; sweat of blood (hematidrosis). "Then His sweat became like great drops of blood falling down to the ground." (Luke 22:44).

Case not usual in medical practice. In arising it is associated to blood disorders.

Physiologically it is due to capillary vascular congestion and hemorrhages in the sweat glands. The skin becomes fragile and tender. After this first situation caused by the intense anguish he is subjected to a fast that lasts all night during the trial and will persist until his crucifixion.

FLOGGING

Flogging was a legal prerequisite for all Roman execution. The victim's upper part of the body was stripped naked, chained to a pillar not very high, with his back hunched, so that the unloading of the beating, lost no force and whipping without compassion, without any mercy. The usual instrument was a short whip (flagrum or flagellum) with several ropes or leather cords, which had tied small iron balls or small pieces of bones of sheep at various intervals. When soldiers beat repeatedly and with all their strength the backs of their victim, the iron balls caused deep bruises and hematomas. The leather cords with the sheep bones, tore the skin and the subcutaneous tissue. On continuing the whipping, the lacerations cut as far as the muscles, producing bloody strips of torn flesh. The conditions were created to produce important loss of fluids (blood and plasma). It is necessary to bear in mind that the hematidrosis had left the skin sensitive in Jesus.

After the flogging, the soldiers used to mock their victims. Jesus, was placed a crown of thorns on his head, as an ironic emblem of his royalty. In Palestine there are many thorny shrubs, which could serve for this purpose; they used the Ziziphus or jujube, called Spina Christi, of long sharp thorns. A robe was placed over his shoulders (an old soldier's robe, contained the purple of which the kings, "Scarlet Chlamys"), and a reed, similar to the rush of Cyprus and of Spain as a scepter in his right hand.

CRUCIFIXION

The ordeal of the cross is of oriental origin. It was received from the Persians, Assyrians and Chaldeans; by the, Greeks, Egyptians, and Romans. It was modified in several ways over the course of time. In the beginning, it was a simple post. Then a scaffold (furcal) was fixed at the top, from which the suspended the prisoner by the neck. Then adding a cross stick (*patibulum*), taking a new look. According to the way in which the cross stick shall be subject to the vertical mast, three kinds of crosses originated:

1.-The *crux decusata:* Known as the cross which had the form of an X.
2.-The *crux commissata*: This had the form that looked like the letter T.
3.-The *crux immisa*: It is the so-called Latin cross, we all know.

Forced to Jesus, as it was customary to carry the cross; from the post of flogging to the place of crucifixion. The cross weighed more than 300 pounds (136 kilos) only took the *patibulum* that weighed between 75 and 125 pounds. It was placed on his neck and dangled on his two shoulders.

With weakened and extreme exhaustion, he had to walk a little more than a mile (between 600 to 650 meters) to reach the site of the torture. The name in Aramaic is Golgotha, equivalent in Hebrew *gulgole*t, which means "Place of a Skull", since it was a rocky lump, which had some resemblance with a human skull, today is called by the Latin translation Calvary.

Before the torture of crucifixion, it was customary to give a narcotic drink (wine with myrrh and incense) to convicted persons; in order to mitigate their pain a little. When this mixture was introduced to Jesus, he would not drink it. What could mitigate a moral and physical pain so intense, when his entire body, all bruised, only waiting to face his last torture, no relief whatsoever, with full control of himself?

With arms extended, but not tense, wrists were nailed on the scaffold. In this way, the nails of one centimeter in diameter on its head and of 13 to 18 centimeters long, were probably placed between the radius and the metacarpal, or between the two rows of carpal bones, either near or through the strong flexor retinaculum and several intercarpal ligaments. In these places they secured the body.

The placing of the nails in the hands would make it tear easily since they did not have an important bone support. The possibility of a painful periosteal wound was large, as well as the injury of tributary arterial vessels of the radial or ulnar artery. The penetrated nail destroys the motor sensory nerve, or compromised the median, radial or ulnar nerve. The effect of any of these nerves produced tremendous shocks of pain in both arms. The impalement of several ligaments caused strong contractions in the hand. The feet were set in front of the stipe by a nail of iron, riveted through the first or second intermetatarsal space. The deep peroneal nerve and ramifications of the median and lateral nerves of the sole of the foot were injured.
Were both feet nailed with a single nail or a nail for each foot? This is also a

controversial issue. But it is much more likely that each one of the feet of the Savior was attached to the cross with different nail. Cyprian that, more than once had witnessed crucifixions, speaks in the plural of nails which pierced the feet and many others expressly mention the four nails used to crucify Jesus.

Melitón of Sardis wrote: "the physical suffering already so violent in having driven in the nails, in organs extremely sensitive and delicate, was made even more intense by the weight of the body suspended from the nails, by the forced immobility of the patient, by the intense fever that was ensuing, by the burning thirst produced by this fever, by the convulsions and spasms, and also the flies that the blood and sores attracted."

There have been those who said that the Savior's feet were not nailed, but simply subject to the cross with ropes; but such hypothesis has against, both the unanimous testimony of the tradition, which sees in the crucified Jesus the fulfillment of that, famous prophecy: "They have pierced my hands and feet." (Psalm 21); as in the Gospels themselves, as we read in Luke (Luke 24:39-40) “Look at my hands. Look at my feet. You can see that it's really me. Touch me … As he spoke, he showed them his hands and his feet.”

Bosssuet says: how to describe the moral sufferings that our Lord Jesus Christ endured during his horrific agony? When a crowd of people satisfied their eyes with the spectacle of that agony, accompanied with all kinds of outrages that filled him until the last moment. He suffered at see the selfless gaze of his mother and his friends, to whom their pains had plunged into deep sadness. All He was, let's say it this way, a torment in his members, in his spirit, in his heart and in his soul.

Of all the deaths the cross was the most inhumane, degrading torment, which was reserved for slaves in the Roman Empire (*servile suppliciun*). After the words in Gethsemane come the pronounced in the Golgotha, which attest to this depth, unique in the history of the world. "My God, my God, why have you abandoned me?" His words are not just expression of that neglect, they are words repeated in prayer and that are found in Psalm 22.

Pathophysiological Interpretation of the Death of Jesus Christ

The death of Jesus several factors could contribute. It is important to note that it was a person poly-traumatized and poly-contended; from the moment of the flagellation, to his crucifixion. The main effect of the crucifixion, apart from the tremendous pain, presented in his arms and legs, was the marked interference with normal breathing, particularly in exhalation. The weight of the body pulled down, with arms and shoulders extended, tended to establish the intercostal muscles to a state of inhalation and consequently affecting the passive exhalation. In this way the exhalation was first of all diaphragmatic and the respiration very light. This form of breathing was not sufficient and would soon produce, retention of CO^2 (hypercapnia). To be able to breathe and get air Jesus had to rely on his feet, trying to bend his arms and then let it collapse so exhalation occurs. But being collapsed equally produced a series of pain throughout his body. The development of muscle cramps or tetanic contractures due to fatigue and hypercapnia affected even more the respiration. An adequate exhalation required that the body by pushed upwards with the feet and bending the elbows, creating adduction in shoulder. This maneuver would bring the total weight of the body in the tarsals and cause tremendous pain. Moreover, flexion of the elbows will cause rotating wrists around the iron nails and cause enormous pain through torn nerves. The raise of the body painfully scrape his back against the stipe. As a result every effort of breathing would become agonizing and tiring, eventually leading to suffocation and finally his death.

It was the custom of the Romans that the crucified bodies remain long hours hanging from the cross; sometimes until they entered in putrefaction or wild beasts and birds of prey devoured them. Therefore before Jesus died, the princes of the priests and the Sanhedrin colleagues asked Pilate that, according to Roman custom, to order to finish off the executed person, having the legs broken with beating. This barbaric operation was called in Latin *crurifragium* (John 20:27). The legs of the thieves were broken, additionally when getting to Jesus and observing that he was already dead, they gave up striking him. But one of the soldiers for greater security wanted to give what is called the "coup de grace" and penetrated the chest with a spear.

In this blood and in that water that came out of the side, the doctors have concluded that the pericardium, (saclike membrane that surrounds the heart), had been reached by the spear, or it caused perforation of the right ventricle or perhaps had a post-traumatic haemopericardium, or represented fluid of pleura and pericardium, from where the bloodshed would have proceeded. With this analysis that although it is a conjecture, brings us closer to the real cause of his death. Interpretations that are inside a scientific rigor in terms of its theoretical part; but not demonstrable with analysis nor complementary studies. The changes suffered in the humanity of Jesus Christ, have been seen in the light of medicine, in order to really find the human character, in a man that is called the son of God, and that voluntarily accepted this torture, convinced in the redeeming and saving effect for those that believe in Him and in his Gospel

BIBLIOGRAPHY

New Living Translation Bible. 2005 Tyndale House Publishers, Inc.

Holman Dictionary. 2008 B&H Publishing Group.

Dictionary.com. 2011. Larousse Editorial.v

Made in United States
Orlando, FL
29 October 2022

23984200R00057